Athena GCSE Guide to Edexcel IGCSE English Language A

Table of contents	Page
Introduction	2
PART ONE: PROSE And POETRY TEXTS	5
1.1 Introducing Prose Texts: *Significant Cigarettes*, from The Road Home	7
1.2 'Whistle and I'll Come for You' from The Woman in Black	15
1.3 *Night*	23
1.4 *The Necklace*	34
1.5 *The Story of an Hour*	44
1.6 Introducing Poetry Texts: *The Bright Lights of Sarajevo*	50
1.7 *Disabled*	63
1.8 *An Unknown Girl*	72
1.9 *Out, Out-*	78
1.10 *Still I Rise*	84
PART TWO: IMAGINATIVE WRITING	89
2.1 Personal Writing: Narrative Perspective	91
2.2 Imaginative Writing: Setting and Plot	105
2.3 Imagined Experiences: Developing Dialogue	116
2.4 Developing Narrative	136
2.5 Writer's Toolkit	153
GLOSSARY OF TERMS	160

Who is this study guide for?

This Study Guide is designed to help the IGCSE English Language learner explore a range of poetry and prose fiction texts. It will support the consideration and understanding of the ways in which writers use narrative and descriptive techniques to capture the interest of readers. The learner will then demonstrate their own narrative and descriptive skills in an imaginative writing response to a written prompt, scenario or image.

This Study Guide is intended to support learners who undertake a GCSE qualification in English Language following the **Edexcel IGCSE English Language Specification A (4EA1)**, with a particular focus on the skills required for **Paper 2: Poetry and Prose Texts and Imaginative Writing.**

This Study Guide will also help to lay a sound foundation for those who go on to study English at Advanced level, as well as appeal to those who are interested in developing their general literacy skills.

This Study Guide focuses on Imaginative Reading and Writing, using fiction texts from 19th, 20th and 21st century sources. There is a companion Athena IGCSE Guide for Paper 1, which provides a focus on Non-Fiction Texts and Functional Writing. The Paper 2 guide aims to develop reading and writing skills using non-fiction texts from the 19th, 20th and 21st centuries.

Links to Examination and Assessment

This Study Guide has been designed to be used as a study aid in order to support learners in attaining a qualification in the following examined unit:

**4EA1 Edexcel International GCSE in English Language 4EA1/01
Paper 2: Poetry and Prose Texts and Imaginative Writing**

GCSE English Language Paper 2: How is reading assessed?

Reading and writing are given equal importance on the GCSE course. Reading is assessed on both of your examination papers. Edexcel IGCSE English Language A Paper 2 is titled **Poetry and Prose Texts and Imaginative Writing.**

In Paper 2 Section A, you will be asked to show that you can:

- Understand prose and poetry texts, choosing parts that are relevant to certain ideas.

- Explain how writers use language, style and form to create specific effects for the reader.

The English Language GCSE examination does require some preparation of active reading and writing skills. As it uses anthology texts, your preparation and skills development will be critical in supporting you to demonstrate your knowledge and understanding of these texts in the examination.

You will be expected to:

- Recognize and gather information and meaning from texts
- Select, examine and evaluate what is relevant
- Understand and explain implicit (embedded or hidden) meanings and attitudes
- Appreciate how writers achieve effects within text

The source for the Paper 2 reading questions will be the **Edexcel IGCSE English Language Anthology Section B.** The texts are from two genres: poetry and prose fiction. Source materials include poems and extracts from novels and short stories. These extracts will provide a focus on one or more of the following: openings, endings, narrative perspectives and points of view, narrative or descriptive passages, character, atmospheric descriptions and other relevant narrative and descriptive approaches.

In this paper, you will be asked to response to one text from the Edexcel anthology. You may be asked to explore how the writer presents a theme or character, or how that moment is made significant or moving for the reader. Responses should include a discussion of how language and form are used to convey ideas.

Where possible, there should be some appreciation of when a text was written and where the narrative is set. Attitudes and values vary over time and can vary from culture to culture, and from place to place. In the examination, you may be presented with a passage or a short story from different time periods, or a passage written in English but originating in a particular country or culture.

GCSE English Language Paper 2: How is writing assessed?

For Section B of Paper 2, learners will be required to craft a piece of imaginative writing in response to a selected task. In this response, the learner will be expected to write imaginatively, and to provide effective and clear communication. Work will be assessed on the ability to:

- Write effectively and coherently using the appropriate register, vocabulary, grammar and linguistic conventions

Structure of Assessment

Paper 2 is worth **40%** of the total IGCSE grade. Examinations are available in January and June.

Section A Non-Fiction Texts: Candidates provide an extended response to a selected poetry or prose text from Part 2 of the Pearson Edexcel International GCSE Anthology. Total for Section A: 30 marks.

Section B: Imaginative Writing: One imaginative writing task from a choice provided. Total for Section B: 30 marks.

It is suggested that 45 minutes is spent on Section A, and 45 minutes spent on Section B. A copy of the anthology will be provided in the examination.

Using this Guide

This guide provides support for reading poetry and prose anthology texts, using these texts to provide ideas for narrative and descriptive writing. Section A of the guide aims to develop analytical skills when reading. The first section of the guide includes analysis of the set extracts from the poetry and prose section of the Edexcel Language anthology.

This guide will support you in meeting the aims and objectives of the Edexcel IGCSE English Language qualification, enabling you to:

- Read a wide range of texts fluently, and with understanding
- Read critically
- Use knowledge of wider reading to inform and improve your own writing
- Write effectively and coherently using the appropriate register, vocabulary, grammar and linguistic conventions

Part One of this GCSE Guide will provide detailed analysis of the Section 2 poetry and prose texts from the Edexcel anthology, accompanied by questions to direct the reading and exploration of themes. You will need to have access to a copy of the Edexcel IGCSE anthology when responding to Part One tasks.

Throughout the guide, exam-style questions will be used to enable you to gain practice at responding to other unseen extracts.

Part Two of the guide will support the development of imaginative writing skills. Suggested responses to reading and writing tasks are also provided throughout the guide.

Young boy working with buzzsaw

PART ONE: Prose and Poetry Anthology Texts (Paper 2 Section A)

1.1 Introducing Prose Texts: *Significant Cigarettes, from The Road Home:* Reading Prose
1.2 *'Whistle and I'll Come for You' from The Woman in Black*
1.3 *Night*
1.4 *The Necklace*
1.5 *The Story of an Hour*
1.6 Introducing Poetry Texts: *'The Bright Lights of Sarajevo'*
1.7 *Disabled*
1.8 *An Unknown Girl*
1.9 *Out, Out-*
1.10 *Still I Rise*

Paper 2 Poetry and prose texts and Imaginative writing (40%)

Section A- Poetry and prose texts 20%

The focus of this section of the guide is reading and understanding a range of prose and poetry texts. Students will need to be familiar with all the texts in Section B (Part 2) of the **Pearson Edexcel International GCSE English Anthology**.

There will be a single essay question, worth 30 marks, based on one of the **Part Two Pearson Edexcel International GCSE English Anthology** texts.

In each section of the first part of this guide you will:

- carry out a close reading of the poem or prose extract
- understand the wider context of the anthology text
- understand the content, including unusual vocabulary
- analyse the structure of the poem or prose text
- analyse the style of the text
- understand the theme(s) the author is writing about
- prepare for writing about the anthology extracts in your exam

1.1 Introducing Prose Texts: *'Significant Cigarettes'* from *The Road Home* by Rose Tremain

This section will help you to;

- *Read and understand a variety of texts*
- *To selecting and interpret information, ideas and perspectives*
- *Understand and analyse how writers use linguistic and structural devices to achieve their effects.*

GCSE English Language: How is reading assessed?

Reading and writing are given equal importance on the GCSE course. Reading is assessed on both of your examination papers. Edexcel IGCSE English Language A Paper 2 is titled **Poetry and Prose Texts and Imaginative Writing.** In Paper 2 Section A, you will be asked to show that you can:

- Understand prose and poetry texts, choosing parts that are relevant to certain ideas.
- Explain how writers use language, style and form to create specific effects for the reader.

The English Language GCSE examination does require some preparation of active reading and writing skills. As it uses anthology texts, your preparation and skills development will be critical in supporting you to demonstrate your knowledge and understanding of these texts in the examination.

You will be expected to:

- Recognize and gather information and meaning from texts
- Select, examine and evaluate what is relevant
- Understand and explain implicit (embedded or hidden) meanings and attitudes
- Appreciate how writers achieve effects within text

The source for the Paper 2 reading questions will be the **Edexcel IGCSE English Language Anthology Section B.** The texts are from two genres: poetry and prose fiction. Source materials include poems and extracts from novels and short stories. These extracts will provide a focus on one or more of the following: openings, endings, narrative perspectives and points of view, narrative or descriptive passages, character, atmospheric descriptions and other relevant narrative and descriptive approaches.

In this paper, you will be asked to response to one text from the Edexcel anthology. You may be asked to explore how the writer presents a theme or character, or how that moment is made significant or moving for the reader. Responses should include a discussion of how language and form are used to convey ideas.

Where possible, there should be some appreciation of when a text was written and where the narrative is set. Attitudes and values vary over time and can vary from culture to culture, and from place to place. In the examination, you may be presented with a passage or a short story from different time periods, or a passage written in English but originating in a particular country or culture.

Chapter overview

In section 1 of the guide you will be responding to the poems, short stories and extracts from novels presented in the Edexcel anthology, and complete different types of revision tasks. Some tasks will be essentially **'reading for information'** and will support the development of your skimming and scanning skills. The processes of skimming and scanning are outlined below.

The second type of task requires **'reading for meaning'**. Here you will form your own opinion about a piece of literature and look for evidence in the text to support your views. There will be some questions that ask you to think about language choices and how these affect meanings. As you move through the guide, you will be supported in developing your close reading skills.

Active vs. passive reading

Reading is very much a part of our everyday life, and often unfamiliar words can be read without really thinking about meaning. If we are reading something in which most of the text is recognisable, we tend to gloss over anything that is new in a process termed *passive reading*. Examples of passive reading can include reading emails, watching credits on television programmes, and glancing at text messages.

Active reading involves a process where you have to pause and reflect on what you are reading, perhaps because the topic covered is new to you or the ideas presented in the text are complex and challenging. Active reading is a skill that can be developed. Active reading is necessary both for adult literacy and for this qualification, as throughout the IGCSE you will be required to engage in reading for understanding.

Much of our reading now takes place on social media platforms and via web-based texts. Often, our encounters with extended literary texts also take place via electronic platforms such as Kindle or iBooks. This presents a particular set of challenges, as often we have to scroll through information rather than turning the page of a book or newspaper. For those students who wish to continue study in English Language beyond GCSE, comparison of print and multimedia texts forms part of the A Level syllabus.

Skimming and scanning

When you are presented with an unseen text in exam conditions, using reading skills such as skimming and scanning can help you read for overall meaning and respond briefly to questions about the way ideas are presented in the text.

Section A of Paper 2 will require you to **SKIM** (read quickly for the gist or main idea of the passage or extract) and **SCAN** (look carefully for certain information) a set text from Section B of the Edexcel IGCSE English anthology. The exam paper will suggest how many minutes you should spend re-reading the text.

Using Reading Time: Skimming and Scanning a text

- Skim through the whole text, scanning for any words that are unfamiliar, and see if you can work out the meaning of them.

- RE-read the ending and be sure of what it says.

- Read through the text again, looking at how it is structured and how the paragraphs or verses are linked.

- Look again at the opening (the title and first paragraph, or the opening lines of a poem). How does it work as an introduction?

- Look at the reading question. It may include bullet points or key words that will tell you what to focus on. Make sure you understand what is required.

- Go back to the text and mark up the sections that you need. Then you can begin your response.

'Significant Cigarettes' from *The Road Home* by Rose Tremain: Background Context

Rose Tremain (1943-) is a British author who has had numerous novels published. She writes on a wide range of subjects and is well-known for her historical novel *Restoration*. In this extract from *The Road Home* the reader is given a description of the experiences of Lev, a migrant, who travels to England from Eastern Europe in search of work to support his mother and young daughter.

Content

In this passage Lev has set off from his home and is on the early part of his journey in the coach where he talks to fellow-passenger, Lydia, about their reasons for heading to England. He reflects back on his wife, who has recently died, and his young daughter and mother, whom he has left behind. The novel and to some extent the extract explore his homesickness, and the balance between his aspirations and anticipation of a new life, and the loneliness and loss felt as he leaves his family behind him.

Task: Searching for Symbolism

Food is a very important motif or symbol in the novel.

How does Tremain illustrate Lev's journey in terms of food?

You should consider:

- The first references to food in the passage
- How Lydia's lunch prompts a memory
- Why Lev seems to favour smoking rather than eating

Suggested Response to Task: Searching for Symbolism

You may have noticed the first reference to food seems off-putting. As Lev considers the long coach journey, he seems uncomfortable at the thought of sharing '*smells of food*' with the passenger next to him.

Tremain provides a detailed description of Lydia's snack as she prepares her egg sandwich. The reference to rye bread provides a cultural context in terms of food which may remind Lev of home. As Lydia peels the cold egg, Lev finds the smell reminds him of sulphur. Again, this seems unpleasant, with possible associations with Hell, suggesting this trip is painful for him. The sensory description is ambiguous, as the smell does then remind him of a trip he took with his wife to some sulphur springs. It is a bittersweet memory – the smell was unpleasant and the water *'scummy'* but Marina did notice a stork's nest, and this image has stayed with him, as he has learnt the phrase in English.

Throughout the extract Lev shows no interest in food but seems to desperately crave smoking. He does have a small drink of vodka from a flask, but vows not to join other men in drinking when he arrives in England. It may be that in the past he has chosen to eat little or not at all at times when he has struggled to provide meals for his daughter. The extract also suggests smoking has become an activity in itself, a way he keeps himself company and an excuse for remaining isolated. In this way the cigarettes are 'significant'. The lack of food and constant smoking have taken their toll, leaving a 42 year old man *'grey'*.

Structure

The extract is presented from a **third person, omniscient perspective** but we see everything from Lev's point-of-view and he is the **focaliser** for the events that follow. The text guides the reader through the situations encountered on his journey towards England.

The passage opens with Lev sitting at the back of the coach to England *'huddled against the window'*. He looks at *'the land he was leaving'*. There is a sense of decay in the *'fields of sunflowers scorched by the dry winds'*, but also a natural beauty in the *'wild garlic growing green'*. The **alliteration** used in these descriptions highlights these contrasts. The author then proceeds to present Lev and Lydia and their initial exchange about his cigarette.

Lev is not yet 43 yet he does not seem healthy, his face *'grey-toned from his smoking'*. Lydia is described as a *'plump, contained person'*. He is keen to co-operate when she reminds him the coach has a no-smoking policy, yet it is a sign of Lev's loneliness that he craves a cigarette, as *'even an unlit cigarette was a companion'*.

Lev then reflects on the strange situation of being in such close proximity to a stranger and thinks of the journey ahead. They will sit *'side by side with their separate aches and dreams, like a married couple'* yet when they reach London will go their own way with *'barely a word or a look'*. Lev is not naïve; he knows life in a new country will be hard and if able to find a job *'he would break his back working'*. He plans to stay separate from others. He does not need to belong to a group as long as he can *'sit and smoke'*. Lev feels if he can do this he can show *'his heart remained in his own country'*.

The writer then describes the practical aspects of the journey; the need for two coach drivers to take turns driving as it will take 50 hours, the onboard toilet and the stops for gas at service stations, which will allow passengers a short break to stretch their legs and see *'flowers on a verge, soiled paper among bushes'*. The focus would seem to shift to Lev on a break, who would *'smoke and stare at the cars rushing by'*. The description seems bleak and reflects Lev's impatience with a journey which seems *'to have no end'*.

Lev cannot manage to sleep sitting up, as at 42 he is *'not yet old'*. He sees sleeping upright as a skill of the elderly, which brings to minds his father Stefan. He recalls sleeping with his father on hay and the forest floor, and sleeping on the rug next to his daughter's bed when she was ill. His final memory recalls lying on hospital lino beside the bed of his wife Marina as she was dying.

The smell of Lydia's egg as she eats a snack recalls a trip to the sulphur springs, taken as a desperate hunt for an alternative cure for his wife. There is a bitter tone as he remembers the *'scummy water'* but he also recalls his wife wishing she could be a stork as *'you never see a stork dying'*. The style of the extract shifts from use of description and the character's internal reflections to present dialogue, as Lev strikes up a conversation with Lydia where we get to know more about each character.

Lydia reveals she is travelling for an interview as a translator in London. She has left a job teaching in Yarbl. Lev is curious about why she would leave a job behind and she explains that she was *'tired of the view from my window'*. She is frank in her desire not to *'die seeing these things'*. There is silence as Lydia eats before Lev asks her to help with his pronunciation. His words show the type of interactions he anticipates; *'Lovely. Sorry. I am legal. How much please. Thank you. May you help me.'*

Lydia corrects his final phrase, although it might be argued he is more in need of help than being able to provide it at this point. It is a sign of the importance of his wife's memory that he has learnt the English words for *'Stork. Stork's nest'*. Lydia corrects *'Bee and Bee'* before realising he means B and B, a form of lodging.

As night falls, Lev vows his heart will always hold the way dusk arrives in his home, Auror. He shares a little of his life with Lydia, how he lost his job two years ago when the town mill ran out of trees and closed, and how his mother has supported him and his daughter by making and selling tin jewellery. The author implies these memories are painful, as Lev then takes out a flask of vodka, and is described at feeling guilty about his own reflection in the window, as after his wife Marina's death he holds his *'own guilt at still being alive'*.

When Lydia asks about other work, he shows an imaginative side, as he pictures groups of young men, *'industrious immigrants'*, living together and making their own vodka while watching television each night after work. This seems a friendly picture but Lev wishes to remain alone as *'England is my hope'*. He needs to earn money to send home and he cannot afford to make friends or become distracted by other people.

Lydia falls asleep and we return to Lev alone again as night approaches. He cannot sleep and joins the bus driver in a *'lonely, exhausting vigil'*. He is becoming restless, and is attempting to divert himself from his craving for a cigarette, *'nicotine or oblivion'*. He carefully studies a £20 note. There is a suggestion of comedy in his description of the *'frumpy queen'*. He assumes that the image of a *'personage from the past'* -actually Elgar, a famous composer -is that of a banker, and seems puzzled to find it on the note. He has been taught *'The British venerate their history'*, even when some *'past deeds were not good'*.

This leads Lev to another imaginative reflection. He reads the dates of the man's life, 1857-1934, and decides he is a capitalist banker who did not have to suffer the cruelties Hitler or Stalin, as he died in 1934. This implies the depth to which Lev's own country suffered due to these two men.

Lev suggests that the 1929 Wall Street Crash would have been simply *'a little loss of capital'* to his imagined banker, even though he has been taught men jumped from skyscraper windows due to the broken economy. As a man who died before the bombing of London or the devastation of Europe during the Second World War, Lev decides that this man must have had luck in his life – *'it was known across the world: The English were lucky'*. His final reflection in the extract sees him strike a defiant tone and affirm that he was going to England was *'going to make them share it with me: their infernal luck'*. 'Infernal' is an interesting choice of adjective as it has connotations of hell and damnation. Here Lev uses it to begin a bold hope – *'my time is coming'*. It is interesting to note that in the final section, from line 148, the text is more immediate as we hear Lev's voice. The writer invites us to view the world through his eyes as we are told these are his thoughts.

Language

As an extract from a modern novel, this text may appear to use a combination of straightforward language and **colloquial** or informal expression.

On second reading, a number of Tremain's techniques can be identified. She makes use of literary devices such as **alliteration, repetition** and **listing** to make the familiar new or strange.

In the sequences of dialogue, when Lev tries to speak to Lydia using his English phrases the reader recognises that he has some issues associated with additional language learning. They may see this as a way of foreshadowing potential communication problems that lie in store when he reaches England.

The repeated references to food, drink and cigarettes make these items significant or **symbolic** (the extract and chapter bear the title 'Significant Cigarettes'). When combined with the explicitly political references to '*Capitalism*', '*Hitler*' and '*Stalin*' they too become political and suggest that the narrative may be driven by the 'culture clash' that Lev will experience on arrival. He does not seem to desire to go to England, but feels forced there as a way of earning enough money to support his mother and his daughter.

1.2 *'Whistle and I'll Come for You'* from *The Woman in Black* by Susan Hill

This section will help you to;

- Read and understand the anthology extract 'Whistle and I'll Come for You' from The Woman in Black by Susan Hill
- To selecting and interpret information, ideas and perspectives
- Understand and analyse how writers use linguistic and structural devices to achieve their effects.

Evoking Atmosphere

The prose extract used in this section provides an interesting example of a modern text which is written to evoke or create a specific atmosphere.

The writer Susan Hill (1942-) is a successful English author who has published a wide range of novels and non-fiction. The novel from which the extract is taken, *The Woman In Black*, is a modern writer's re-working and re-imagining of a Victorian ghost story. Hill skilfully using suspense and an ominous atmosphere to sustain tension and create a dramatic impact. The themes of the novel are present in microcosm in this extract. These include fear and the supernatural, reality versus imagination and the mystery of the unknown.

In the full extract, subtitled *'Whistle and I'll Come to You'*, the narrator, a solicitor named Arthur Kipps, recounts his experiences as a young man. He had been called upon to sort out the papers of a recently deceased woman. The isolated situation of the woman's house required him to remain there overnight, unaccompanied.

Structure and Style

Throughout his stay in the house, Kipps suffers a horrifying sequence of unexplained noises, disturbing events and eventual apparitions of the cursed `Woman in Black'. The title of the extract is not only a chapter of the novel, but is also the title of the Victorian ghost story which inspired Hill's tale. In the original version, an arrogant man is tormented by spirits who are summoned by a whistle.

Task: Building Atmosphere

Read the section taken from the anthology extract 'Whistle and I'll Come for You', re-printed below:

1. Look at the way Arthur Kipps describes the wind at the start of the chapter.
2. How does Hill use pathetic fallacy to convey his memories?
3. How does Hill build tension in the opening section of the chapter?

Taken from 'Whistle and I'll Come to You' from *The Woman in Black* by Susan Hill

During the night the wind rose. As I had lain reading I had become aware of the stronger gusts that blew every so often against the casements. But when I awoke abruptly in the early hours it had increased greatly in force. The house felt like a ship at sea, battered by the gale that came roaring across the open marsh. Windows were rattling everywhere and there was the sound of moaning down all the chimneys of the house and whistling through every nook and cranny.

At first I was alarmed. Then, as I lay still, gathering my wits, I reflected on how long Eel Marsh House had stood here, steady as a lighthouse, quite alone and exposed, bearing the brunt of winter after winter of gales and driving rain and sleet and spray. It was unlikely to blow away tonight. And then, those memories of childhood began to be stirred again and I dwelt nostalgically upon all those nights when I had lain in the warm and snug safety of my bed in the nursery at the top of our family house in Sussex, hearing the wind rage round like a lion, howling at the doors and beating upon the windows but powerless to reach me. I lay back and slipped into that pleasant, trancelike state somewhere between sleeping and waking, recalling the past and all its emotions and impressions vividly, until I felt I was a small boy again.

Then from somewhere, out of that howling darkness, a cry came to my ears, catapulting me back into the present and banishing all tranquillity.

I listened hard. Nothing. The tumult of the wind, like a banshee, and the banging and rattling of the window in its old, ill-fitting frame. Then yes, again, a cry, that familiar cry of desperation and anguish, a cry for help from a child somewhere out on the marsh.

There was no child. I knew that. How could there be? Yet how could I lie here and ignore even the crying of some long-dead ghost?

'Rest in peace,' I thought, but this poor one did not, could not.

In your response to the task, you may have noted that **pathetic fallacy** is employed at the start of the passage, when the wild weather is described and sharply contrasted with the memories Kipps holds of being wrapped up in bed as a child. Writers often use this technique to create a particular atmosphere and guide the reader's responses.

Suggested Response to the Task: Building Atmosphere

'Whistle and I'll Come to You' is a chapter which makes great use of pathetic fallacy as it describes heavy winds on a stormy night. Hill presents the reader with a description of the storm, as experienced by Kipps. Nature seems out of balance as *'The house felt like a ship at sea'*. **Similes** are used to convey the dramatic nature of the storm. Kipps tries to reassure himself, reasoning that the house has survived many storms and is as *'steady as a lighthouse'*.

The extract may remind the reader of other ghost stories. There is the suggestion of the supernatural. As Kipps struggles to sleep he hears *'Windows rattling'* and *'the sounds of moaning down all the chimneys'*. The wind is also compared to a banshee, a ghostly vision from Irish tradition which is an omen warning of death. This prepares the reader for the later apparition.

There is a shift in **tone**, as Kipps recalls feeling safe in his childhood home during a storm. **Simile** is used as he recalls how *'the wind raged round like a lion, howling at the doors and beating upon the windows but powerless to reach me.'*

The third paragraph consists of a single, **complex sentence**, which builds tension through multiple clauses, before introducing the eerie cry, *'banishing all tranquillity'*. As Arthur is alone, there are only three words which appear as direct speech, *'Rest in Peace'*. The reader is unsure if these words are thoughts or have been spoken aloud as Arthur addresses the ghost.

Task: Endings - Whistle and I'll Come for You

The following text is from the ending of the extract. How has the writer structured the text to interest you as a reader?
You could write about:

- what the writer focuses your attention on as the chapter concludes
- how and why the writer changes the focus from the rescue of Spider to the apparition in the window
- any other structural features that interest you.

Once again it was a noise that had awakened me. Spider was scratching and whining at the door and I realized that it was some hours before the poor creature had been let out. I got up and dressed briskly, went downstairs and opened the front door. The sky was swollen and streaked with rain clouds, everything looked drab and without colour and the estuary was running high. But the wind had died down, the air was lighter and very cold.

At first the dog trotted across the gravel toward the scrubby grass, anxious to relieve herself, while I stood yawning, trying to get some life and warmth into my body by beating my arms and stamping my feet. I decided that I would put on a coat and boots and go for a brisk walk across the field, to clear my head, and was turning to go back into the house when, from far out on the marshes, I heard, unmistakably clean and clear, the sound of someone whistling, as one whistles to summon a dog.

Spider stopped dead in her tracks for a split second and then, before I could restrain her, before I had fully gathered my wits, she set off, as though after a hare, running low and fast away from the house, away from the safety of the grass and out across the wet marshes. For a few moments I stood amazed and bewildered and could not move, only stare, as Spider's small form receded into that great open expanse. I could see no one out there, but the whistle had been real, not a trick of the wind. Yet I would have sworn it had not come from any human lips. Then, even as I looked, I saw the dog falter and slow down and finally stop and I realized in horror that she was floundering in mud, fighting to maintain her balance from the pull beneath her feet. I ran as I have never run before, heedless of my own safety, desperate to go to the aid of the brave, bright little creature who had given me such consolation and cheer in that desolate spot.

At first the path was firm, though muddy, beneath my feet and I could make good speed. The wind coming across the estuary was bitingly cold on my face and I felt my eyes begin to smart and water, so that I had to wipe them in order to see my way clearly. Spider was yelping loudly now, afraid but still visible, and I called to her, trying to reassure her. Then I, too, began to feel the stickiness and the unsteadiness of the ground as it became boggier. Once I plunged my leg down and it stuck fast in a watery hole until I managed to exert all my strength and get free. All around me the water was swollen and murky, the tide of the estuary was now high, running across the marshes themselves, and I was obliged to wade rather than walk. But at last, out of breath and straining with every movement, I got almost within reach of the dog. She could scarcely hold up now, her legs and half her body had disappeared beneath the whirling, sucking bog and her pointed head was held up in the air as she struggled and yelped all the while. I tried two or three times to stride across to her but each time I had to pull free abruptly for fear of going under myself. I wished that I had got a stick to throw across to her, as some sort of grappling hook with which to grab hold of her collar. I felt a second of pure despair, alone in the middle of the wide marsh, under the fast-moving, stormy sky, with only water all around me and that dreadful house the only solid thing for miles around.

But aware that, if I gave into panic, I should most certainly be lost, I thought furiously and then, very cautiously, lay down full length on the marsh mud, keeping my lower body pressed as hard as I could onto a small island of solid ground and, reaching and stretching my trunk and my arms forward, inch by inch, gasping for breath until, just as the last of her body sank, I lunged out and grabbed the dog about the neck and hauled and strained and tugged with all the force I could, a strength I would never have dreamed I could have summoned up, born of terror and desperation; and after an agonizing time, when we both fought for our lives against the treacherous quicksand that tried to pull us both down into itself and I felt my grip on the slippery wet fur and wet flesh of the dog almost give, at last I knew that I would hold and win. I strained as hard as ever I could to drag my body backward onto firmer ground. As I did so, the dog's body suddenly gave and the tug of war was over as I fell back, holding her tight, the two of us soaked with water and mud, my chest burning and my lungs almost bursting, my arms feeling as if they had been dragged from their sockets, as indeed they almost had.

We rested, panting, exhausted, and I wondered if I would ever be able to get up, I felt suddenly so faint and weak and lost in the middle of the marsh. The poor dog was making choking noises now and rubbing her head against me over and over, no doubt both terrified and also in great pain, for I had nearly asphyxiated her as I had clutched so hard around her neck. But she was alive and so was I and, gradually, a little warmth from each of our bodies and the pause revived us and, cradling Spider like a child in my arms, I began to stumble back across the marshes toward the house. As I did so and within a few yards of it, I glanced up. At one of the upper windows, the only window with bars across it, the window of the nursery, I caught a glimpse of someone standing. A woman. That woman. She was looking directly toward me.

Spider was whimpering in my arms and making occasional little retching coughs. We were both trembling violently. How I reached the grass in front of the house I shall never know but, as I did so, I heard a sound. It was coming from the far end of the causeway path which was just beginning to be visible as the tide began to recede. It was the sound of a pony and trap.

Suggested Response to Task: Endings

Tension returns through Spider's actions, as the dog begins *'scratching and whining at the door'*. The reader is relieved when Kipps indicates this is simply because the dog wants to be let out. Just as the reader relaxes a whistle is heard and it is *'not from any human lips'*.

The **pace** and tension reach almost unbearable levels as Kipps tries desperately to rescue Spider from the mud. The choice of **verbs** highlight the panic - the dog *'yelped'* and *'struggled;* Kipps uses all of his strength to rescue the dog from the *''whirling sucking bog'*. Hill's choice of **adverbs** *'furiously'* and *'cautiously'*, and range of dynamic verbs, as Kipps *'lunged'*, *'grabbed'*, *'hauled'*, *'tugged'* Spider create a frantic pace, whilst the adjectives describing the marshland and mud as *'treacherous'*, *'agonizing'* and *'slippery'* reinforce the sense of imminent threat. Kipps' physical isolation suggests he is powerless against the evil which surrounds the house.

When Kipps eventually frees Spider, Hill employs **tri-colon listing** to highlight the physical pain felt by Kipps: *'chest burning, lungs almost bursting, my arms feeling as if they had been dragged from their sockets'*.

The reader tries to relax and recover with Kipps at this point before Hill's delivers the chilling twist of the chapter. As Kipps, looks back towards the house and sees *'A woman. That woman. She was looking directly towards* me.'* The use of **short, sharp sentences** are used to support the link between what happened to Kipps and the appearance of the ghost.

It is at this point, when the reader has been mollified by the narrow escape that Hill delivers the shocking climax:

'At one of the upper windows... I caught a glimpse of someone standing. A woman. That woman. She was looking directly towards me.'

Short sentences replicate the breathlessness of Kipps at this point. The reader is forced to slow down. This in turn causes them to focus more closely on what is being read and also emphasises the significance of the moment.

No description of the woman is required. Hill does not need to say more to achieve the effect— the reader understands and joins Kipps in his trepidation in these few short phrases.

The vital difference to the other times that he has sensed the presence of the woman is that she is now looking directly at him. presenting him with a challenge or a threat.

Hill then escalates the terror at the very end of the chapter by introducing the sound of the *'pony and trap'*. Both Kipps and the reader feel sensory over-load. From a narrative perspective, Hill has linked the sounds and the sight of the woman together in the climax of the extract.

Structure and Style

Despite Hill's assertions that this was neither Gothic or a ghost story, the style of the extract follows many of the conventions of the typical Gothic novel.

Pathetic fallacy is employed at the start of the passage, when the wild weather is described and sharply contrasted with the memories Kipps holds of being wrapped up in bed as a child.

The following paragraph consists of a **single, complex sentence** paragraph, which builds tension through multiple clauses, before introducing the eerie cry of a child. As Arthur is alone, there are only three words which appear as direct speech. The reader is unsure if these words are thoughts or have been spoken aloud as Arthur addresses the ghost.

The older narrator still has difficulty trying to articulate his understanding of the events or to explain rationally what was happening that night. In a typical horror trope (extended metaphor), towards the end of the experience he is left in total darkness.

Throughout the passage, multiple descriptive clauses are contrasted with short sentences and rhetorical questions to effectively convey the thoughts churning through young Arthur's mind.

Given the nocturnal setting, many of the verbs used make reference to sounds, while the imagery can be categorised into light and dark. A sense of foreboding is created in the description of oppression and other negative responses.

Task: Evaluating Writer's Craft – 'Whistle and I'll Come for You'

Look at the way Hill builds tension and creates a sense of Arthur's fear at the end of the chapter.

- How does Hill use pathetic fallacy to convey his memories?
- How does Hill build tension in the closing section of the chapter?
- How does Hill use a variety of sentence structures to convey Arthur's responses?
- What is the significance of the sound of the pony and trap approaching?

Suggested Response: Evaluating Writer's Craft

Here is an example of how you might comment on Hill's use of language. It refers to the end of the chapter and the dramatic confrontation with the woman in black. It begins with Arthur Kipps' relief that he has found the dog alive.

'But she was alive and so was I and, gradually, a little warmth from each of our bodies and the pause revived us and, cradling Spider in my arms like a child, I began to stumble back across the marshes towards the house.'

It is at this point, when the reader has been mollified by the narrow escape that Hill delivers the shocking climax:

At one of the upper windows... I caught a glimpse of someone standing. A woman. That woman. She was looking directly towards me.'

Short sentences replicate the breathlessness of Kipps at this point. The reader is forced to slow down. This in turn causes them to focus more closely on what is being read and also emphasises the significance of the moment.

No description is required. Hill does not need to say more to achieve the effect— the reader understands and joins Kipps in his trepidation in these few short phrases.

The vital difference to the other times that he has seen the woman is that she is now looking directly at him. presenting him with a challenge or a threat.

Hill then escalates the terror at the very end of the chapter by introducing the sound of the pony and trap. Both Kipps and the reader feel sensory overload. From a narrative perspective, she has linked the sounds and the sight of the woman together in the climax of the extract.

Marshlands

1.3 *Night* by Alice Munro

This section will help you to;

- Read and understand the prose short story Night by Alice Munro
- To selecting and interpret information, ideas and perspectives
- Understand and analyse how writers use linguistic and structural devices to achieve their effects.

Night Alice Munro: Background Context

The story concerns the darkness of the writer's mind, rooted in the restlessness experienced as a young girl recovering from an operation. The story is part of a final quartet in Alice Munro's short story collection *Dear Life*. Munro (1931-) calls the quartet of stories 'a separate unit, one that is autobiographical in feeling, though not, sometimes entirely so in fact'. In the past, Munro created distance between her writing and her own experience. Here, the stories have some grounding in events that have taken place in her life, although she has added fictional elements.

Content

'Night' presents a story inspired by Munro's insomnia as a child on her family farm in Ontario. Sleeping above her younger sister, the narrator is alarmed by thoughts of strangling her in the night. In an attempt to avoid causing harm, she begins to walk outside the house and in the garden. One evening she meets her father on the porch.

The story is written from a child's perspective and reveals attitudes towards her father's response. Towards the end of the story, she also makes overt comment on parenting as an adult looking back.

Her father does not seem to share mother's disappointment in her and seems to take the role of observer of choices. As an adult looking back, she sees her own actions as a parent as making her *'humbled'* and *'disgusted'*. The father does not feel this. She seems to praise her father yet goes to refer to beatings.

Parents and children are a central theme for Munro. There is shifting importance of time and place in understanding the past. She compares the parenting philosophy at the time when the story was set and at the time of writing. In addition to the presentation of family relationships, the story is interested in psychological health and the differences between past and present.

Analysis of *Night*

As the story begins, the narrator associates all disasters in life with snowstorms. The narrator sees herself as *'touched by death'*. Her mother seems careless in her revelation of the *'turkey's egg growth'* which was removed from the narrator's body during an operation for appendicitis in childhood. This growth may or may not have been cancer. The word remains unspoken yet alters the child's character.

She begins her night walks as a way of seeking peace, after the shocking confession that she has to drive away thoughts of harming her younger sister. There seems to be a gradual decay in life which is a result of her own poor health. The night becomes a symbol of her illness and isolation from her family and the world. She seeks meaning by walking in nature.

In the closing sections of the story she is offered alternatives to what is happening in her mind. Some consider this to be a weak ending. While based on events in her own life, Munro writes the story as fiction. She saw her father's woes as too many to be credible; it *'wouldn't do in fiction'*.

First-person narrative

When presented with a **first-person** narrative, which conveys the story from the **perspective or point of view** of the narrator, consider how the writer engages the reader with the narrator's thoughts and experiences. As a reader, do you sympathise with this character? You should identify and evaluate the literary and linguistic methods that the writer has used to convey thoughts and emotions. For example, complex sentences and multiple clauses may indicate that a character is confused or trying to make sense of a situation.

The opening below is from *Private Peaceful* by Michael Morpurgo. Notice how the writer creates a mystery with the speaker's words. The language is quite straightforward but builds a sense of tension. Why is this night 'far too precious'? We learn the narrator is not yet eighteen. There is a sense of foreboding as they wish the night to be 'as long as my life' and do not want to 'rush' towards dawn. Even if you have not read the book you may guess the fate of the young person who desires to 'feel alive'.

> *They've gone now, and I'm alone at last. I have the whole night ahead of me, and I won't waste a single moment of it. I shan't sleep it away. I won't dream it away either. I mustn't, because every moment of it will be far too precious.*
>
> *I want to try to remember everything, just as it was, just as it happened. I've had nearly eighteen years of yesterdays and tomorrows, and tonight I must remember as many of them as I can. I want tonight to be long, as long as my life, not filled with fleeting dreams that rush me on towards dawn.*
>
> *Tonight, more than any other night of my life, I want to feel alive.*
>
> From *Private Peaceful* by Michael Murpurgo

In this section of the guide, you will undertake a series of tasks using extracts from the short story *Night* by Alice Munro. Written in first person, *Night* presents a story inspired by Munro's insomnia as a child on her family farm in Ontario. Unable to sleep, the narrator is alarmed by thoughts of strangling her sister in the night. In an attempt to avoid causing harm, she begins to walk outside the house and in the garden. One evening she meets her father on the porch and tells him her fears. The story is written from a child's perspective, though the narrator later reveals her adult feelings about her father's response.

Narrative Perspective

The story is presented as a first-person narrative. The extract takes us from the narrator's account of her appendicitis operation, which also removed a tumour, through to her return home and the sleepless nights tormented by what she may do to her sister with a series of short paragraphs highlighting her fear. The writer uses **direct address** (speaking directly to the reader) a number of times to pull the reader into her story. By writing in this way, Munro invites the reader to think about whether the girl has overcome her difficulties.

> **Task: Reading for Understanding**
>
> **How does the writer present differing attitudes towards the tumour or 'growth' in the extract below?**
> You should consider the words and phrases used.

Reading for Understanding

...Then I went back to school, and enjoyed being excused from physical training for longer than necessary, and one Saturday morning when my mother and I were alone in the kitchen she told me that my appendix had been taken out in the hospital, just as I thought, but it was not the only thing removed. The doctor had seen fit to take it out while he was at it, but the main thing that concerned him was a growth. A growth, my mother said, the size of a turkey's egg.

But don't worry, she said, it's all over now.

The thought of cancer never entered my head and she never mentioned it. I don't think there could be such a revelation today without some kind of question, some probing about whether it was or it wasn't. Cancerous or benign – we would want to know at once. The only way I can explain our failure to speak of it was that there must have been a cloud around that word...

So I did not ask and wasn't told and can only suppose it was benign or was most skilfully got rid of, for here I am today. And so little do I think of it that all through my life when called upon to list my surgeries, I automatically say or write only 'Appendix'. ...In the heat of early June I got out of school, having made good enough marks to free me from the final examination. I looked well, I did chores around the house, I read books as usual, nobody knew there was a thing the matter with me.

Suggested Response to the Task: Reading for Understanding

At first, the narrator's mother seems awkward and reluctant to introduce the tumour, using the word *'it'*. Long after her return from hospital, the narrator's mother tells her that her appendix *'was not the only thing removed'*.

Having been so reluctant to discuss it, her mother now seems careless in her revelation of the *'turkey's egg growth'* which may or may not be cancer. The word 'cancer' remains unspoken between them yet alters her character.

As an adult looking back, the narrator now realises that there should have been a discussion about the health implications, yet at the time her mother was keen to move on without further discussion and tells her not to worry as *'it's all over now'*.

Although the narrator does not explicitly say so, there is an implied link between this and her later psychological anxieties. She insists *'so little do I think of it'*, yet realises there was a *'failure to speak of it'*. The narrator seems to want to repress the experience and notes how she returned to her normal activities and *'nobody knew there was a thing the matter with me'*.

Structure and style

'*Night*' has a loose structure. Munro uses this to explore final taboos. The story is typical of Munro's style in the use of plain prose style. The narrative provides a full description of the world at night-time. The use of words with negative connotations reflect her mental instability.

There is a sense of the **gothic** in the nocturnal setting. The story also provides a meditation on the origins of fiction. In her darkest time, the teenage narrator asked herself '*Why not try the worst?*'

Alice Munro's family home

Of course there were no streetlights – we were too far from town.

Everything was larger. The trees around the house were always called by their names – the beech tree, the elm tree, the oak tree, the maples always spoken of in the plural and not differentiated, because they clung together. Now they were all intensely black. So were the white lilac tree (no longer with its blooms) and the purple lilac tree – always called lilac trees not bushes because they had grown too big.

The front and back and side lawns were easy to negotiate because I had mown them myself with the idea of giving us some townlike respectability. …

Back and forth I walked, first close to the house and then venturing here and there as I got to rely on my eyesight and could count on not bumping into the pump handle or the platform that supported the clothesline. The birds began to stir, and then to sing – as if each of them had thought of it separately, up there in the trees. They woke far earlier than I would have thought possible. But soon after those earliest starting songs, there got to be a little whitening in the sky. And suddenly I would be overwhelmed with sleepiness. I went back into the house, where there was suddenly darkness everywhere, and I very properly, carefully, silently, set the tilted chair under the doorknob, and went upstairs without a sound, managing doors and steps with the caution necessary, although I seemed already half asleep. I fell into my pillow, and I woke late – late in our house being around eight o'clock.

Task: Close reading: *Night*

Look in detail at the extract above:

How does the writer use language here to describe the narrator's 'night walks'?

You could include the writer's choice of:

- **words and phrases**
- **language features and techniques**
- **sentence forms**

Suggested Response to the Task: Close Reading

The setting of the story at night is also **symbolic**. It represents the remoteness from family, of isolation from life in general. The extract begins by stating this isolation; *'Of course there were no streetlights – we were too far from town.'* Night is used by the narrator to protect herself and her family, while she tries to find meaning in life by looking at nature in its nocturnal state. There is **personification** in her description of the maples; *'they clung together'* as she seems to attribute her insecurity to the trees. Despite her negative thoughts she can see life and hope in the world outside her house. She marvels at the birds, who start to sing one by one, *'as if each of them had thought of it separately'*. She is surprised at their early start but it seems linked with a glimmer of hope or positive thought, as she notices *'a little whitening in the sky'*.

The writer makes use of **complex** sentences and lengthy sentences, as the narrator tries to respond to nature and clear her mind. This contrasts with the **adverbial clause** *'And suddenly'* which marks the end of the walk, as she becomes *'overwhelmed with sleepiness'*. The return to the house marks a sharp **contrast** as *'there was suddenly darkness everywhere'*. The house seems to return her to a negative state of mind. The narrator's caution is highlighted in the **triplet** *'properly, carefully, silently'*, which describes her attempts to stealthily re-set the chair against the door. The narrator seems exhausted as she recalls how *'I fell into my pillow'*. The choice of **verb** presents her weakened state.

The narrator is returning from her night walk when she sees her father, sitting dressed in a formal suit. She realises he has heard her outside at night several times.

Task: Endings

The following is an extended extract from the end of the short story *'Night'*.

How has the writer structured the text to interest you as a reader?

How does the narrator feel about her father's response?

I knew now that he had not heard me getting up and walking around on just this one night. The person whose livestock was on the premises, whose earnings such as they were lay all close by, and who kept a handgun in his desk drawer, was certainly going to stir at the slightest creeping on the stairs and the easiest turning of the knob.

I am not sure what conversation he meant to follow then, as regards to my being awake.

He seems to have declared wakefulness to be a nuisance, but was that to be all? I certainly did not intend to tell him more. If he had given the slightest intimation that he knew there was more, if he'd even hinted that he had come here intending to hear it, I don't think he'd have got anything out of me at all. I had to break the silence out of my own will, saying that I could not sleep. I had to get out of bed and walk.

Why was that?

I did not know.

Not bad dreams?

No.

'Stupid question,' he said. 'You wouldn't get chased out of your bed on account of good dreams.'

He let me wait to go on, he didn't ask anything. I meant to back off but I kept talking. The truth was told with only the slightest modification. When I spoke of my little sister I said that I was afraid I would hurt her. I believed that would be enough, that he would know enough of what I meant.

'Strangle her,' I said then. I could not stop myself after all.

Now I could not unsay it, I could not go back to the person I had been before. My father had heard it. He had heard that I thought myself capable of, for no reason, strangling little Catherine in her sleep.

He said, 'Well.'

Then he said not to worry. He said, 'People have those kinds of thoughts sometimes.'

He said this quite seriously and without any sort of alarm or jumpy surprise. People have these kinds of thoughts or fears if you like, but there's no real worry about it, no more than a dream, you could say.

He did not say, specifically, that I was in no danger of doing such a thing. He seemed more to be taking it for granted that such a thing could not happen. An effect of the ether, he said. Ether they gave you in the hospital. No more sense than a dream. It could not happen, in the way that a meteor could not hit our house (of course it could, but the likelihood of its doing so put it in the category of couldn't).

He did not blame me though, for thinking of it. Did not wonder at me, was what he said.

There were other things he could have said. He could have questioned me further about my attitude to my little sister or my dissatisfactions with my life in general. If this were happening today, he might *have made an appointment for me to see a psychiatrist. (I think that is what I might have done for a child, a generation and an income further on.)*

The fact is, what he did worked as well. It set me down, but without either mockery or alarm, in the world we were living in.

People have thoughts they'd sooner not have. It happens in life.

If you live long enough as a parent nowadays, you discover that you have made mistakes you didn't bother to know about along with the ones you do know about all too well. You are somewhat humbled at heart, sometimes disgusted with yourself. I don't think my father felt anything like this. I do know that if I had ever taxed him, with his use on me of the razor strap or his belt, he might have said something about liking or lumping it. Those strappings, then, would have stayed in his mind, if they stayed at all, as no more than the necessary and adequate curbing of a mouthy child's imagining that she should rule the roost.

'You thought you were too smart,' was what he might have given as his reason for the punishments, and indeed you heard that often in those times, with the smartness figuring as an obnoxious imp that had to have the sass beaten out of him. Otherwise there was the risk of him growing up thinking he was smart. Or her, as the case might be.

However, on that breaking morning he gave me just what I needed to hear and what I was even to forget about soon enough.

I have thought that he was maybe in his better work clothes because he had a morning appointment to go to the bank, to learn, not to his surprise, that there was no extension to his loan. He had worked as hard as he could but the market was not going to turn around and he had to find a new way of supporting us and paying off what we owed at the same time. Or he may have found out that there was a name for my mother's shakiness and that it was not going to stop. Or that he was in love with an impossible woman.

Never mind. From then on I could sleep.

Suggested Response to Task: Endings

The narrator has a sudden realisation that her father has been fully aware of her night-time wanderings. The extract provides a **description** of the conversation she has with her father who, although their relationship was clearly not always smooth and easy, calms her. Their conversation is presented mostly without speech marks, with a combination of **direct speech** and the narrator's evaluation of how effective his words are. When she confesses to a desire to strangle her sister he calmly responds *'People have those kinds of thoughts sometimes'*. As an adult she reflects *'There were other things he could have said'*.

Her father does not seem to share mother's disappointment in her and seems to take the role of observer of choices. The father does not feel she has a serious psychological problem, and reassures her that her disturbing thoughts will pass. She seems to praise her father yet goes on to refer to beatings. As an adult looking back, she sees her own actions as a parent as making her '*humbled*' and '*disgusted*'.

Only at the end of the story does she wonder why he himself was up at night dressed in his better work clothes. The mature narrator understands that her father was losing sleep over financial troubles and her mother's failing health. At the end of the story, it seems to be the teenage voice of the narrator refusing to be sympathetic and egotistically referring to her own experience by concluding '*Never mind. From then on I could sleep*'.

Task: Evaluating Writer's Techniques

Re-read the ending of the story '*Night*' used in the previous task.

Some readers have found this a weak ending to the story.

To what extent do you agree?

In your response, you could:
Consider the narrator's response to her father's words.
Evaluate how the writer creates a sense of reflection and looking back.
Support your responses with references to the text.

Suggested Response to Task: Evaluating Writer's Techniques

You might argue that her father is quite passive and unhelpful in the narrative. Much of this text is about what is not said. It could be argued that the series of short questions he asks her are not just 'small talk' but a way of inviting her to share her problems. He is suggesting he will not judge her.

You could argue that the power comes from the trust she puts in her father, in contrast to the ways in which her mother tried to ignore the illness and the impact it had on her mental state. It may be argued that she does not find solace in her father, but still has a moment of epiphany which enables her to project to a future self and therefore overcome her darker thoughts.

Parents and children are a central **theme** for Munro. There is shifting importance of time and place in understanding the past. She compares the parenting philosophy at the time when the story was set and at the time of writing. She does not explicitly judge her mother for not discussing the cancer, suggesting that her approach was a sign of the times. She does not blame her father for his distant relationship with her.

In addition to the presentation of family relationships, the story is interested in psychological health and the differences between past and present. You may have selected a supporting quotation from the following extract, when the narrator describes her father's reaction to her violent thoughts:

'He did not blame me though, for thinking of it. Did not wonder at me, was what he said.

There were other things he could have said. He could have questioned me further about my attitude to my little sister or my dissatisfactions with my life in general. If this were happening today, he might have made an appointment for me to see a psychiatrist. (I think that is what I might have done for a child, a generation and an income further on.)'

One of the striking things about the text is the shock of realising such a young narrator is harbouring homicidal thoughts. You could look at the structure of the story and comment on how the girl begins to walk outside in order to create distance and protect her sister.

You might argue that her father is quite passive and unhelpful in the narrative. Much of this text is about what is not said.

You could argue that the power comes from the trust she puts in her father, in contrast to the ways in which her mother tried to ignore the illness and the impact it had on her mental state. It may be argued that she does not find solace in her father, but still has a moment of epiphany which enables her to project to a future self and therefore overcome her darker thoughts.

In the closing sections of the story the narrator is offered alternatives to what is happening in her mind. Some consider this to be a weak ending. References are made to her father's use of physical violence on his children. The narrator's memories seem vague here and her overall **tone** is positive as she decides *'However, on that breaking morning he gave me just what I needed to hear and what I was even to forget about soon enough.'*

1.4 *The Necklace* by Guy de Maupassant

This section will help you to;

- Read and understand a variety of texts
- To selecting and interpret information, ideas and perspectives
- Understand and analyse how writers use linguistic and structural devices to achieve their effects.

The Necklace Guy de Maupassant: Background Context

The author, Guy de Maupassant (1850–1893), was French, and a major figure in the development of the short story as a literary form. He is known for his clever plotting.

'The Necklace' is set among the French middle classes, who were very anxious to keep up appearances and aspired to be accepted by the social elite. Madame Loisel's proud determination to replace the borrowed diamond necklace she loses at the ball reflects the values of her class and the society in which she lived, as does her husband's initial excitement at being invited to the reception at the Minister of Education's house.

Nineteenth century paste imitation diamond necklace

Task: Reading for Meaning: *The Necklace*

1. How far can you relate to Madame Loisel's fantasies about living a life of upper-class elegance? What do you think of her insistence on having a new dress and jewellery to wear to the reception?

2. How are the main characters revealed in the following lines?

(a) *'she felt that she was intended for a life of refinement and luxury'* (12–13)

(b) *'Ah! Stew! Splendid! There's nothing I like better than a nice stew...'* (line 27)

(c) *'She had no fine dresses, no jewellery, nothing. And that was all she cared about'* (line 33)

(d) *'You'll be able to see all the big nobs there'* (line 48)

(e) *'He was totally disconcerted and dismayed by the sight of his wife who had begun to cry'* (line 52–3)

(f) *'What's up? You haven't half been acting funny these last few days'* (lines 74–5)

(g) *'She danced ecstatically, wildly, intoxicated with pleasure'* (line 108)

(h) *'quickly and heroically, she resigned herself to what she could not alter: their appalling debt would have to be repaid'* (lines 191–2)

3. Maupassant keeps us in suspense for a while after the necklace goes missing, drawing out the process by which the couple come to accept that they must replace it. How does he do this?

Suggested Response to Task: Reading for Meaning

1. Madame Loisel is to some extent a victim of her culture's expectations of women. The question also required you to present your own first impressions of the character.

2. (a) *'she felt that she was intended for a life of refinement and luxury'*
She is a dreamer with rather vain ideas about herself.

(b) *' Ah! Stew! Splendid! There's nothing I like better than a nice stew...'*
He is an uncomplicated man, content with an ordinary life.

(c) *'She had no fine dresses, no jewellery, nothing. And that was all she cared about'*
She is vain and materialistic. She apparently does not care about her husband or family, or about the meaning of life.

(d) *'You'll be able to see all the big nobs there'*
Loisel is an unsophisticated man, with a naïve, lower-class acceptance of authority. He wishes to please his wife, yet he does not understand that seeing 'the big nobs' will not in itself be enough for her.

(e) *'He was totally disconcerted and dismayed by the sight of his wife who had begun to cry'*
He does not understand her dreams and longing for a different life.

(f) *'What's up? You haven't half been acting funny these last few days'*
He cannot read her behaviour, and is more baffled than concerned.

(g) *'She danced ecstatically, wildly, intoxicated with pleasure'*
She is energetic, capable of happiness, albeit of a shallow kind, and she loves attention.

(h) *'quickly and heroically, she resigned herself to what she could not alter: their appalling debt would have to be repaid'*
She has a surprising ability to face a tough situation with resolution and determination. Moreover, she has moral integrity, even if this is based on the conventional outlook of her class.

3. He describes their efforts to find the necklace. Where possible, you should try to quote examples from various parts of the story.

Content

This is a well plotted story with well-defined characters and a great deal of **situational irony**. Like many of the best short stories, it hinges on one key problem – in this case the lost necklace. Loisel is portrayed as rather dull and insensitive, yet a loving and essentially kind-hearted husband. His wife is someone who has dreams of personal grandeur, and who finds her actual situation hard to bear.

Maupassant's comments in the second section reflect commonly held views about women at the time. In an effort to maintain social acceptance Mr and Mrs Loisel embark on a life of penury in order to replace the necklace. The bitter twist at the end of the story is that the piece Mme Loisel has struggled to replace was costume jewellery, made of paste and glass.

Style

Maupassant is very much the **omniscient** author in this story, permitting himself to reveal whatever he likes about the internal lives of his characters. However, he reveals much more about Madame Loisel than about her husband. He gives us insights into her attitude towards her life, and into her fantasy world. When she is forced to accept poverty, Maupassant describes how she becomes a hard, haggling wife out of necessity.

Task: Literary Devices

- One technique Maupassant uses is contrast, sometimes in conjunction with lists of three. Explain how he does this in the opening paragraph.

- Sum up in your own words the content of Madame Loisel's fantasies, shown in Paragraphs 3–4, and how Maupassant's language fits the subject matter.

- The husband's feelings are more often revealed by indications than by direct explanation. How is this done in lines 69, 155 and 181?

- What literary technique is used in line 182, and to what effect?

Suggested Response to Task: Literary Devices

- **One technique Maupassant uses is contrast, sometimes in conjunction with lists of three. Explain how he does this in the opening paragraph.**

He lists three things that Madame Loisel lacked before her marriage: *'no dowry, no expectations, no means of meeting some rich, important man who would understand, love, and marry her.'* The third item on this list (*'no means of meeting some rich, important man ...'*) itself has a sub-clause which is broken down into a list of three. This list of what she lacks is contrasted with what she settles for: a junior clerk. The lengthy list, followed by the contrasting brief, humble actuality, is mildly humorous.

- **Sum up in your own words the content of Madame Loisel's fantasies, shown in Paragraphs 3–4, and how Maupassant's language fits the subject matter.**

She wants a wealthy, indolent lifestyle, with luxury and splendour and influence. She also wants the attention of important men. All this is echoed in the lavish description: *'silent antechambers hung with oriental tapestries, lit by tall, bronze candelabras, and of two tall footmen in liveried breeches ...'* Is it possible that Mme Loisel has been reading sentimental novels? Through Mme Loisel, is Maupassant criticizing this genre, written specifically for women like Mme Loisel, for setting up unrealistic expectations about life? In some ways, Madame is similar to those women today who read about celebrity lifestyles and fantasize about living in this way themselves.

- **The husband's feelings are more often revealed by indications than by direct explanation. How is this done in lines 69, 155 and 181?**

He appears pale and hollow-cheeked and is *'sick with worry'*.

- **What literary technique is used in line 182, and to what effect?**

Personification. Poverty is like a devouring beast, *'ready to pounce'*.

Structure

The story hinges on the loss of the necklace. Most of the account is given over to the reception and the loss of the necklace. The ten years of poverty are dealt with more generally. The story returns to more detailed narrative and dialogue from line 218.

The structural device of **contrast** is used throughout. The story follows the Mathilde Loisel through her life stages: her formative years, married life before the reception, the dramatic crux of the reception, with loss of the necklace. Her later life is shaped by the aftermath; an impoverished life for the next decade; the final meeting at the end of story. The omniscient narrator uses Mathilde Loisel as a **focaliser**, while maintaining an ironic distance. The reader appreciates the irony of how she has believed her life to be hard and less than she deserved. By the end of the story she is truly destitute.

Task: Style in The Necklace

Why does the narrative become more detailed at this point?

How could the story be given a happy ending? For example, what might Madame Forestier do or say on hearing about the necklace?

Do you think the ending is better left as it is, on a note of biting situational irony?

Suggested Response to Task: Style

Why does the narrative become more detailed at this point?

It once again engages us in the immediate drama of dramatic interchange between characters. There is a close focus on the dialogue between Madame Forestier and Madame Loisel, because the all-important twist of the story is about to be revealed.

How could the story be given a happy ending? For example, what might Madame Forestier do or say on hearing about the necklace?

Madame Forestier could say, *'Oh, you poor dear. I'll sell it and give you what I get, minus the 500 francs the original was worth.'* Then the Loisels would have all the money that in effect they had saved up. They could invest it in a business, perhaps one which would enable Madame Loisel to meet rich people. They could make more money, perhaps have children, and live happily ever after.

This might, however, rather spoil the ironic twist of the story and give it a quite different message, in effect rewarding Madame Loisel for her vanity and materialism. This might spoil the moral of the story, which hinges on not wanting things that are beyond our reach in such a way that we can destroy our own happiness and that of those who are near to us.

Do you think the ending is better left as it is, on a note of biting situational irony?

This question requires you to provide your own personal response to the text and, as such, does not have a set response.

Language and Style

In a fictional text such as *'The Necklace'*, there is more focus on character and relationships. For example, we find evidence of the vanity of the young wife, and of her husband's desire to please her. However, here again context is relevant. The society in which Maupassant wrote placed a high value on women looking decorative, and being able to show off their finery. The fact that the main character does not even consider confessing to her wealthy friend and saying, *'Sorry, I've lost your necklace'*, also relates to nineteenth-century French middle-class values.

The story explores the aspirations and ambitions of those who desire social acceptance. On a personal level, it explores human vanity and the price of jealousy. Throughout the narrative themes are highlighted with lexical choices linked to class distinctions, contrasting rich and poor. References to Madame Loisel are infused with negative connotations.

Narrative perspective in *The Necklace* by Guy de Maupassant

The short story is presented by an **omniscient** narrator. The use of **third person** presents an observation of the woman in her situation. Maupassant creates an ironic distance by using descriptions to subtly convey the woman's attitude to her modest station in life.

From the outset, we get a sense that she places great importance of social status and her sense of entitlement and dissatisfaction with her life is conveyed in the insistence that her humble background is an *'error of fate'*. The narrator at first seems to share these values and it is presented as a shame that she is *'pretty'* and *'delightful'*. At first the omniscient narrator would seem to sympathise with Madame Loisel but as the story continues it becomes apparent that it is an exploration of hope and desire versus reality.

Task: Language

- Is there a difference between the language used when Mme Loisel is at the party or dreaming and when the reality of her life is described? Think about the effects of these contrasts.

- How does Maupassant convey character through direct speech?

Suggested Response to Task: Language

The description of the Loisel home as *'ugly'*, *'battered'* and *'run-down'* suggests it is a place of degradation and seems to cast Madame Loisel as a Cinderella. She is envious of the place held by the *'society lady'* and deems herself an equal. Maupassant tells us how she *'dreamed of silent antechambers hung with oriental tapestries'*. She feels her life is deficient and directs some of her frustration towards her husband. This sense of dissatisfaction is emphasised by tri-colon listing and negation, as Madame Loisel is deemed deficient; *'She had no fine dresses, no jewelry, nothing'*.

Her ambitions may seem superficial to the reader. There is a stark contrast between her misery and her husband's contentment. He seems to celebrate and enjoy simple pleasures, finding the stew *'Splendid!'* The use of the exclamation mark underlines his strength of feeling. There is a **juxtaposition** in ideas and lexis, with his simple enjoyment undermined by his wife's unspoken desires for *'exquisite dishes'* eaten at *'elegant dinners'*.

Madame Loisel's one interaction with a lady from the upper echelons of society deepens her frustration. Maupassant uses **asyndetic listing** to emphasise despair, as after every meeting with the woman *'she would weep* *tears of sorrow, regret, despair and anguish'*. The extension of the **tri-colon listing** here adds to the sense that she feels her burden in life is insurmountable.

The reader may question the compatibility of the Loisels and lose sympathy with Madame, as when her husband garners an invitation to a society party she does not celebrate but instead tosses it *'peevishly on the table'*. Maupassant has chosen the verb *'tossed'* to provide a sense of her aggression, while the adverb *'peevishly'* hints at a bad-tempered nature. This is a shock to the husband, who has tried to please his wife and was *'highly pleased with himself'* when presenting the invitation. There is a naïveté in his assumption that she would be *'delighted'* to attend the party and the optimistic verb *'hoped'* serves to further highlight the contrasting natures of husband and wife. The story continues to present this dichotomy of negative and positive as the party draws near.

As you respond to the following task on characterisation, consider the sources of sadness in Madame Loisel's life. You can record responses on a table.

Source of sadness	Textual Evidence	Effect upon character
A commonplace family and humble background	No control as like others *'get themselves born the daughters of very minor civil servants'*	No opportunity of a well-to-do marriage
Appeal and beauty, but broke		Feels tainted and held in low esteem
Feels herself to be ensnared by social status		

Task: Characterisation

Madame Loisel

Why is Mathilde unhappy at the start of the story?

Mr Loisel

- Do you regard Mr Loisel as worthy of pity (pathetic) or as pitiful?

Madame Forestier

- How does she treat Mme Loisel in the story?
- How would you describe her reaction to the late return of the necklace?
- At the end, is she sympathetic or vindictive?

Suggested Response to Task: Characterisation

Madame Loisel: Why is Mathilde unhappy at the start of the story?

Source of sadness	Textual Evidence	Effect upon character
A commonplace family and humble background	No control; like others who 'get themselves born the daughters of very minor civil servants'.	No opportunity of a well-to-do marriage
Appeal and beauty, but broke	'She had no fine dresses, no jewellery, nothing'	Feels tainted and held in low esteem
Feels herself to be ensnared by social status	'she felt that she was intended for a life of refinement and luxury'	She believes that she deserves a 'better' life, with a more elevated social status.

Mr Loisel

- **Do you regard Mr Loisel as worthy of pity (pathetic) or as pitiful?**

This was a personal response question - you may feel he has admirable qualities yet still find him pathetic due to the situation he is placed in, or you may find him weak and pitiful.

Madame Forestier

- **How does she treat Mme Loisel in the story?**

You may feel that she is not consciously cruel to Mme Loisel but just behaves according to class. It is important when reading stories sent in other historical periods to realise that the central figure for criticism in the story is Mme Loisel.

- **How would you describe her reaction to the late return of the necklace?**

Again, this may depend on your perspective. At first she may seem charitable in her apparent understanding. However, in her admission that she shared paste jewellery - with the implication of value judgement on Mme Loisel- she may appear vicious.

- **At the end, is she sympathetic or vindictive?**

Whichever of the alternatives above, you should support your views with evidence from the text.

- **What is the irony of the paste necklace?**

Not only is there the bitter irony that they have made themselves destitute and faced great hardships for the sake of costume jewellery but the paste necklace also symbolises the lack of substance in this society.

The Ending

The reader is brought into the present with an unexpected meeting between Madame Loisel and Madame Forrester, the woman she aspired to be and the instrument of her social decline.

Throughout the story, Mathilde has shown resolve and has worked hard to resolve the debt of replacing the necklace. This life has become a *'torment'*. Maupassant invites the reader to judge Madame Loisel at an ironic distance - her original suffering is related to the *'squalid wallpapers'* and *'hideous upholstery'*; the luxury of each item revealing that Mathilde has a comfortable life and is only suffering from envy and materialistic greed. Her desire to flaunt the necklace places the family in true destitution and she ironically grows from this, becoming *'simple and proud'*. She still has a final section to learn.

1.5 *The Story of an Hour* by Kate Chopin

This section will help you to;

- *Read and understand a variety of texts*
- *To selecting and interpret information, ideas and perspectives*
- *Understand and analyse how writers use linguistic and structural devices to achieve their effects.*

The Story of an Hour by Kate Chopin: Background Context

Kate Chopin (1850-1904) was an American writer. Recurrent themes in her work include women, and their desire for independence.

Task: Reading Predictions

Let's look at the title of this story first, *'The Story of an Hour'*. Does this title give us any clues about what we are going to read?

Think about what the words in the title mean.

Suggested Response to the Task: Reading Predictions

This short task asked you to focus on the title. The words 'story' and 'hour' create an unusual juxtaposition - a story or narrative traditionally unfolds across time yet we are told in advance this is a single hour. It provides a clue to the writing style - the focus will be on describing events and reactions in detail. We predict that there is something very significant about this hour, and that it will herald some type of significant change.

Analysis of 'The Story of an Hour'

Written in 1894, 'The Story of an Hour' relates the situation of Louise Mallard, a woman considered to have weak health, who has been informed that her husband has been killed in a railroad accident.

The reader is told from the outset that Mrs Mallard 'was afflicted with a heart trouble'. Other characters are presented in 'broad strokes' but some inferences can be made. Her sister Josephine tries to be delicate and in doing so fails to communicate the death of Mr Mallard, using 'veiled hints that revealed in half concealing'. There is a sense Josephine and Richard, her husband's friend, are more concerned with Victorian propriety than Mrs Mallard's welfare. Richard seemed to have been in undue haste, rushing to her after a second telegram to avoid her hearing from a 'less tender' friend.

Mrs Mallard seems to break convention and rather than express disbelief begins to cry with 'sudden, wild abandonment'. When left alone, she succumbs to 'a physical exhaustion that haunted her body'. As the story continues, she begins to think of the freedom that now awaits her. Shortly afterwards her husband reappears– he was not involved in the accident after all. In a dark irony, the sudden realisation that her future remains unchanged becomes the cause of her death, as she suffers a heart attack on seeing her husband. The other characters in the story assume she has died from joy at her husband's survival. The story concerns the opposing themes of independence and freedom.

The writing style is highly descriptive; repetition is used at various points in the story to highlight important links to the theme of freedom, as with the focus on words such as 'open' and 'free'. Poetic devices such as alliteration and internal rhyme are also used to underline the key ideas.

As you read, note the contradiction between her natural grief and the words the writer uses to describe the world outside her window, the 'open square and 'delicious breath of rain', which fell on the trees 'all aquiver with the new spring life'.

Despite her heart condition and overwhelming grief, it is noted that Mrs Mallard is 'young'. While her face has been prematurely lined with 'repression' she does possess a 'certain strength'.

In paragraph 9, the reader discovers that Mrs Mallard is engaging in a form of day-dreaming: *She felt something penetrating her consciousness, but she did not know what it was.*

Task: Prediction and Personal Interpretation

Can you predict what is affecting Mrs Mallard? Remember to analyse the writer's craft as you make your predictions. This elusive something was *'creeping out of the sky, reaching toward her through the sounds, the scents, the colour that filled the air'*.

Was it evil (creeping, reaching toward her) or was it good (sounds, scents, colours in air)?

Suggested Response to Task: Prediction and Personal Interpretation

This task required you to make a personal interpretation, supported by evidence from the text. The feeling the character cannot articulate was *'creeping out of the sky, reaching toward her through the sounds, the scents, the color that filled the air'*. There is an ambiguity - a sense of foreboding in the lexical choice of *'creeping'* and the personification of this sensation *'reaching towards her'* yet simultaneously there is a joy present and a sensory awakening as she notices the *'sounds, scents'* and *'color that filled the air'*. You may also have commented on the American English spelling which conveys the wider context of the story.

Further Analysis

Paragraph 10 suggests that her will power is being tested. The reader wonders what could be so terrible that her chest is heaving with apparent fear as *'she was striving to beat it back with her will'*. The author compares her 'will' to something as powerless as her *'two white slender hands'*. This suggests that whatever thought has entered her head, it is ultimately instinctive and powerful.

We learn that the implacable force is freedom. She says *'free'*. Her eyes lose their terror and become *'keen and bright'*. She is now *'relaxed'*. *'Free'* may refer to the freedom from life's pain that her husband has found in death, but it becomes clear that her excitement is because she feels free from the constraints of her marriage.

Mrs. Mallard's feelings are described in paragraph 12 as a *'monstrous joy that held her'*. This is **oxymoronic**. She feels unnatural for finding pleasure in her husband's death but cannot repress these feelings. She welcomes the thought of a long future *'that would belong to her absolutely'*.

In a powerful action, she reaches out to embrace this freedom. She is not bitter as she notes that people can attempt to bend others to their will through both *'a kind act or a cruel intention'*.

The language is straightforward as she contemplates how she had loved her husband *'sometimes'*. She values freedom and self-expression as a more powerful source than the mysterious love.

The reader and Mrs Mallard are brought back into the situation by the attentions of her sister Josephine, who fears her solitary grieving. There is dramatic irony as the reader is aware that she is far from grieving, but is in fact *'drinking in a very elixir of life'*. As her sister reaches out to hold her, she returns downstairs like a *'goddess of Victory'*.

It is at the moment of triumph that the door opens and Brently Mallard returns unharmed, *'amazed'* at the piercing cry which comes from his wife on seeing him alive.

A single sentence concludes and provides the twist in the tale –

'When the doctors came they said she had died of heart disease – of the joy that kills'.

Structure

The story covers just one hour of Louise Mallard's life. The short paragraphs reflect the hectic thoughts of Louise's last hour as she processes the information given to her and her reaction to the 'death'; her husband's unexpected return and her sudden death provide a sharp, unexpected twist at the end.

Task: Literary Devices I

Read the story again and try to fill in the table below with examples of each technique. You may wish to refer to the glossary if you are unsure of any terms used.

Task: Literary Devices II

Narrative perspective

What point of view is this story told from?

Characterisation (table for illustration)

Name	Evidence	Evaluation
Mrs. Louise Mallard		
Brently Mallard		
Richards		
Josephine		

Theme

What theme would you say represents this short story?

Suggested Responses to Task: Literary Devices I and II

What should have become evident when evaluating narrative perspective is that although there is an omniscient authorial perspective, this is very much an early modernist text, as the reader moves from observing Mrs Mallard from a distance, to joining her in her solitude, to joining the onlookers as they observe her shocking response to her husband's miraculous return.

It can be argued that Mrs Mallard is the **focaliser**, as we are invited to perceive events from her position. There will be further work on narrative perspective in the second section of the guide, as part of the support for your individual writing.

The characterisation task required you to find evidence of characterisation and use it to complete the table. You may have commented on the use of 'flat' characters, or the lack of significance of other characters beyond imparting information or moving the narrative forwards.

The question on theme requires you to evaluate what you think the writer's intention may be. You may wish to consider how your own views of Louise Mallard shifted and changed as the story progressed. How does Chopin's writing style contribute to this development of attitudes?

This activity was designed as an independent learning task to enable you to use both your own response to reading and the notes from the guide to identify and comment upon the literary techniques present in Chopin's story. You may wish to record your response in note form, using a table like the one presented below.

Technique	Quote and Effect upon the Reader
Foreshadowing (hints toward events)	*Knowing that Mrs. Mallard was afflicted with a heart trouble, great care was taken to break to her as gently as possible the news of her husband's death.* **Effect:**
Symbolism (objects use to represent something)	
Irony (outcome is different than expected)	*When the doctors came they said she had died of heart disease – of the joy that kills'.* **Effect:**
Metaphor(comparison)	
Simile (comparison using like or as)	
Personification (human characteristics to an object)	
Alliteration (repetition of consonant sounds at the start of word)	

1.6 *The Bright Lights of Sarajevo* by Tony Harrison: Reading Poems

This section will help you to;

- Read and understand the poem 'The Bright Lights of Sarajevo'
- To selecting and interpret information, ideas and perspectives
- Understand and analyse how writers use linguistic and structural devices to achieve their effects.

Introduction to poetry texts

The following sections of the guide will help you develop your skills in reading and analysing poetry texts. Once you understand the overall meaning and message of each poem, you will practise selecting specific points for your response and identifying supporting quotations. You will primarily focus on how writers use language, style and poetic forms.

In your poetry response you will demonstrate many of the skills that you will have used when writing about your prose texts. You will need to discuss how form, structure and language convey meanings to the reader.

This section provides a brief overview of some features to look for when responding to poems. The remainder of Section A of the guide will support your reading of the anthology poems, with accompanying tasks and extended writing suggestions.

Feedback will be provided on potential interpretations of the poems so you may check your responses.

As you read each poem, think about:

- WHAT language choices and literary devices have been used
- WHY the poet has chosen these techniques
- HOW the reader may respond to choices.

In the examination, making notes around the clean copy of the poem, or annotations, will help you explore the text in a short space of time. You can develop a code as you prepare your revision notes – question marks for difficult words or phrases that you may need to explore, circling or highlighting striking images or examples of figurative language.

Analysing a poem

There are six key steps in working with a poem for the first time:

1. Identify the **SUBJECT** of the poem e.g. 'The poem is about a painful childhood memory'.
2. Identify the **MODE OF ADDRESS** – is it first person ('I'), second person ('you') or third person ('he/she/it'). Also consider who it is addressing – a lover, a family member, the reader...
3. Identify **THEME** or **MESSAGE** – this will reveal the purpose of the poem. It may create an emotional response or convey an opinion about something. There may be more than one aim.
4. Identify **MOOD** of the poem. Think about the various emotions or feelings that are conveyed. What is the general atmosphere?
5. Identify **TECHNIQUES** uses by the poet. This will include poetic devices such as metaphor and alliteration, imagery, structure and form.
6. Include your **RESPONSE** as a **READER**. This is your evaluation of the poem's effectiveness and your consideration of ways that it can be interpreted.

One of the most challenging aspects when reading poetry is identifying poetic techniques in a new text. There are a few features that are easy to look out for on first reading.

Modes of address: The use of first person

When a poem presents the event or subject from a character's point of view it makes use of **first-person perspective**.

When the character seems to be addressing the reader or another audience beyond the frame of the poem the form is known as **dramatic monologue**. First person is used to encourage the reader to share in the personal feelings of the speaker, rather than just witness events. It can add impact to the poem as the reader is made to respond to the events and emotions directly.

Forms of poetry

Some poems follow a very strict pattern. One of the most common forms you may encounter is the SONNET.

Features of a sonnet:

The sonnet has traditionally been used to express love, although modern versions challenge this as an elevated subject. A number of poets in the First World War used the sonnet to express their love for country or respect for the sacrifice made by those who died.

A sonnet has **14 lines**, normally written in **iambic pentameter** (this is an unstressed followed by a stressed syllable – **de-DUM/de-DUM**, etc.)

Shakespearean sonnets consist of **three** stanzas of four lines (**quatrains**) rhyming **ABAB**, followed by a **rhyming couplet** at the end which clinches the argument.

Other poets use the older form of the Petrarchan sonnet, which splits the poem into **eight lines** presenting the argument, followed by **six** leading to a resolution, rhyming **ABBA ABBA**, then **CDCDCD**.

In following these strict patterns, poets have to choose words carefully to fit the rhythm and rhyme scheme of the sonnet form they have adopted.

Free verse

When a poem does not have a recognisable pattern, it does not necessarily mean it has 'no form'. Poets actively choose to avoid rhyme or patterns to convey ideas relating to their theme. Poems written like this are described as being written in **free verse.**

It is worth considering why the poet has chosen to do this. The uneven structure can be used to suggest uncertainty or a lack of control over a situation. It could be that the poet is trying to create a sense of impressions or unrelated memories. Poems exploring personal feelings often use free verse. Another way it can be used is to suggest the passion or uncontrollable emotions of the speaker or subject, as they cannot contain their words within given forms.

Couplets and closing lines

The last two lines of a Shakespearean sonnet rhyme and are called a **rhyming couplet**. They often provide a summing up of the argument presented. The reader expects a resolution when they encounter the rhyming couplet.

Conversely, some poems end in a surprising way. The final lines may suggest uncertainty or ambiguity which leaves the reader questioning the outcome of the poem, or forces them to reflect upon the themes.

Opening lines

Just as closing lines have an expectation of resolution, so opening lines can set the tone of the text and create expectations for subject matter and theme. It is important that you comment on the impact of the opening line of any unseen poem.

Layout

Layout of the poem can be closely related to messages and themes. The indentation of certain words and lines can indicate their significance as turning points within the poem. Used in an extreme form, in shape poems, the lines resemble the subject.

Poetic Devices

Repetition

Repetition of particular words and phrases can emphasise their importance to the overall message. It can also be used to suggest lack of change, so when the phrase finally alters, a transformation has occurred.

Enjambment

When a sentence or phrase runs over from one line to the next or one verse to the next it is known as enjambment. This creates a sense of spontaneous speech or thought. It can also have the opposite effect, slowing down the pace as the speaker or subject gradually remembers or reflects upon events or emotions.

Rhyme and rhythm

Rhyme can be used to highlight thoughts and emotions. It can add urgency to a lover's plea. Repeated rhymes increase the reader's sense of expectation, as they want the completion of each rhyme.

When a poem is largely unrhymed, the introduction of rhyme in one part, such as choosing to end with a rhyming couplet, emphasises the contrast between the feelings being expressed.

Rhythm and regularity force certain words to call attention to themselves, emphasising the emotions of the speaker or poet.

Use of short words can add pace to a poem, particularly with those poems expressing anger or bitterness.

Changes in rhythm and stanza length throughout a poem can allow more detail to be used. It can also reflect a turning point in the narrative.

If a poem uses mainly regular rhythms and then deviates, this can suggest strong emotions which are hard to suppress. Faster rhythms can suggest panic or fear, while a sudden breakdown of the rhythm of the poem can suggest that the speaker or poet can no longer contain their emotions within the poetic form.

Imagery

Imagery appeals to the reader's senses and aid description of concrete or abstract subjects. A number of poems at GCSE use natural imagery when describing human behaviour or feelings, suggesting that certain things are instinctual. Often this is achieved through comparisons using **similes**, likening an object or person to something else using 'like' or 'as', and **metaphors**, were something is said to be something else. When this idea is carried through a poem it is known as an **extended metaphor**.

The opposite effect is achieved when a poet employs **personification**. Here an inanimate object or thing is written about as if it is a human.

Unusual vocabulary

Unusual or striking words force the reader to reconsider a subject. Writers may use dialect, a variation of language from a particular place or background, or archaic language, deliberately using words that are out of use and seem old-fashioned or 'Biblical' to a modern reader to convey the reader to another place and time.

Alliteration may also draw attention to the descriptions of people and things and at times may contribute to reflecting the content of the poem.

Metaphorical or figurative language can help may the reader see something in a new light. Words may have many connotations, or associated meanings, which open certain lines and phrases to a range of interpretation.

This more complex use of language allows the poem's meaning to be explored beyond simple narrative.

Mood

The choice of vocabulary can often help to establish a mood. Descriptive words such as adjectives or adverbs may offer quite telling details about the subject matter.

Certain descriptions of settings can guide the reader's expectations. This is particularly true of the technique used when poets use the natural world and environment to reflect the emotions of speakers or subjects. This is known as **pathetic fallacy**. It is a technique still used in horror films, when events often unfold on dark, stormy nights.

Some settings become **symbolic** within cultures. Spring, for example, is often read as a symbol of growth and regeneration.

Mood can also be created through tone or connotations. For example, if a love poem uses religious language, as in the sonnet in Shakespeare's play *Romeo and Juliet* when the two lovers first meet, this suggests both intensity of passion and a sincere faith in the love.

Irony

Sometimes the mood can be at odds with the language. **Irony** is when one thing is said but its opposite is meant. Irony can be used to show pain, bitterness or sorrow, as the speaker or poet of experience identifies a tension between reality and how we describe it.

When this irony turns bitter, the poet or speaker can be said to be using **sarcasm**. This is bitter and vitriolic and is usually indicated by use of **hyperbole**, or exaggerated language or imagery. Sarcasm can be effective when it shocks the reader into realising the gap between reality and ideals.

To gain your grade in your IGCSE you will also need to read the meanings that lie below the surface, known as the IMPLIED MEANINGS or CONNOTATIONS. You will develop understanding of these throughout the unit.

Approaching the poem

The first poem you will look at is a modern poem. You should try to expose yourself to a range of poetry, as this unit intends to do. To prepare for the examination and gain confidence in reading poetry, try to read:

- Poems in different forms
- Different styles of writing
- Poems written in English but exploring cultures of various countries
- Modern poetry
- Poems from the late 19th and early 20th century (e.g. War poets)

Surface meanings

Before you can begin to analyse specific textual details, you should demonstrate understanding of the 'surface', or 'literal' meanings of texts.

TASK: Surface meanings

Read the poem *The Bright Lights of Sarajevo*. What do you think it is about?

Look at the title. What clues does it give you about the subject of the poem or the ideas it will address?

Having read the poem through again, complete the sentence below.

On the surface, *The Bright Lights of Sarajevo* is about….

Support your interpretation with one quotation from the text.

Suggested Response to Task: Surface Meanings

You may have discussed whether you think this is a love poem or a poem about conflict. You may have decided that it is a poem about love in a time of conflict. If you had no knowledge of the context, the title *'The Bright Lights of Sarajevo'* may have suggested a poem celebrating the glamour and excitement of a large city. The term 'bright lights' is used as an idiom or **synecdoche** of city life, and was often linked to New York and the idea of moving to a city to start a new life.

The Bright Lights of Sarajevo: Background Context

Tony Harrison (1937-) is a British poet and playwright. He wrote this poem as a form of war correspondence for *The Guardian* newspaper during the Bosnian war in the 1990s, which was fought between the Serbs and Croats who lived there.

Content

In the poem Harrison presents the carnage and destruction that war has brought to the city, while describing how the young people of Sarajevo continue to meet each other in the dark and start romantic relationships, in defiance of the terror and violence that rages around them. Thematically he juxtaposes the carnage of war with the hope and resilience of love.

Structure

He presents the poem as one long stanza. The poem is constructed with a series of linked clauses that form **rhyming couplets**. The pattern of the rhyme reflects the pairing of the young men and women of Sarajevo.

There is also a steady rhythm and combined with the frequent use of enjambment, this would serve to mimic the natural speech patterns.

Style

The opening image of the queue outside the bread shop is reprised in a shocking manner later in the poem when Harrison reveals how a similar queue was attacked and massacred. The reader is reminded of the poem's status as **reportage**. It refers to real events in the recent past.

Harrison is known for his manipulation of **colloquial** forms and here uses simple expressions with relatively few examples of figurative language. The lack of poetic devices serves to emphasise the everyday nature of the horror and perhaps suggests that we have become desensitised to suffering in the age of modern warfare.

Not only was this conflict a brutal civil engagement with the horrific practice of ethnic cleansing, state sanctioned genocide on religious grounds, but it was also a conflict with global military intervention in the shape or airstrikes, which did create further civilian casualties. Harrison alerts the reader to some of the impact of this conflict, while **lexical choices** relating to darkness and light connote a battle of good and evil.

Task: Evaluating Effects upon the Reader

Contrasts are made between the beauty of the natural world (the sky) and the man-made destruction below. This further highlights the manufactured nature of evil and the more positive, natural behaviour of the teenagers as they seek each other out in the dark.

Using the grid below, select some examples of crafted language from the poem and comment on how Harrison's use of language shapes the reader's response.

Technique	Example from poem	Effect upon Reader
Colloquial (informal) vocabulary and phrasing		
Shocking or poignant imagery		
Repetition of words or phrases		
Sound effects/ tone/ mood		

Suggested Response to Task

Technique	Example from poem	Effect upon Reader
Colloquial (informal) vocabulary and phrasing	*when a girl's dark shape is fancied by a boy's.*	The is a contrast between the colloquial '*fancied*', a term associated with teenage hormones and lust, and the war-torn conflict zone described around them.
Shocking or poignant imagery	*...where, in 1992/ Serb mortars massacred the breadshop queue/ and blood-dunked crusts of shredded bread/ lay on this pavement with the broken dead.*	The poet shocks the reader by reminding them that the shellholes represent loss of civilian life - the horrific description 'the blood-dunked crusts' and the rhyming of 'bread' with 'broken dead' help the reader imagine the carnage.
Repetition of words or phrases	*the young go walking at stroller's pace,... All take the evening air with stroller's stride*	The teenagers seem oblivious to the tension and destruction around them - the repetition of '*stroller*' indicates they are trying to engage in a romantic walk, despite the fact they are in the dark of an imposed curfew.
Sound effects/ tone/ mood	*the splintered Pleiades, sprinkled on those death-deep, death-dark wells splashed on the pavement by Serb mortar shells.*	Throughout the poem the 's' sound is repeated but it is not always a gentle sibilance and at times is more reflective of the hiss of the shells as they make their way to a target. This contrasts with alliteration on 'd' which here creates a stark effect.

Detailed Notes on *The Bright Lights of Sarajevo*

The **enjambment** between lines 1 and 2 makes the events witnessed sound like the citizens are out enjoying themselves, while the start of line 2 reveals these people are *'queuing'* for basic provisions.

The poet notices they carry *'empty canisters of gas'*. Gas is needed for heat and cooking and seems to be in short supply. There is an incongruous image as he watches them wheeling the gas home in *'prams'*. Instead of young families walking babies, the streets are full of people struggling to have a normal existence.

There is a constant irony undercutting the title *'Bright Lights'*, which normally suggests a bustling and lively city.

Harrison chooses his **adjectives** carefully. The bread is *'precious'* as all have to make do with small portions *'meagre'* grams of bread. The verb *'rationed'* has associations with war and basic survival. Harrison reminds the reader of the lethal threats to safety as the people frequently end up *'dodging snipers'* on their way home.

The poem reads like a list with **anaphora** in the use of *'or'* and *'of'*. This serves to increase the sense of their despair and struggle. There are many hardships the people of Sarajevo face on a daily basis.

Alliteration is used to show the poet's surprise as he reveals he had expected the city to be *'devoid/ of people walking streets Serb shells destroyed'*. The dash at the end of verse 1 indicates a change in tone and outlook.

Verse 2 opens with signs of hope. The onlooker now observes *'The young'*. Although the streets are in total darkness, the teenagers and young adults seem relaxed as they walk *'at a stroller's pace'*.

'Black shapes' emerge and while this image would normally suggest sinister shadows and threats, here the darkness protects them. In a country where people have been executed for their religion, the darkness now makes it impossible to tell the difference between *'Muslim, Serb or Croat'*. The rhyme is telling here (*'mark'/'dark'*), with *'mark'* suggesting a marksman and reminding readers that there are snipers ready to shoot yet the *'dark'* providing the young population with protection and opportunities to meet and mingle.

Harrison uses language to indicate what seem like superficial differences between communities. The reader questions why someone could possibly die because their word for bread is *'hjleb'*, *'hleb'* or *'kruh'*. The sad reality is that language will reveal the community each teenager belongs to and could prove fatal. Harrison dispels this tension by once again remarking on the *'stroller's stride'*. The youth of Sarajevo seem to be enjoying themselves as the poet uses a deliberately archaic phrase, as they *'take the evening air'*. This seems a fitting way to describe the confidence and pace of the young walkers.

In this section of the poem the city is no longer threatening but a zone for play and flirtation. The reader cannot relax completely, as the poet uses language to allude to the ongoing threat. As the girl tries to make out the features and voice of the boy, she becomes a *'tender radar'*. Here the juxtaposition of technical and military jargon with expressions of love is a stark reminder of the couple's surroundings.

Voice is used to show approval and the scene resembles a Shakespearean courtship. In the darkness a *'match or lighter'* is used to see each other's eyes and establish whether attraction is mutual. The poet presents the unknown couple as a modern Romeo and Juliet.

The reporter poet now watches a couple who have moved beyond the *'match-flare test'*. He keenly observes them walking hand in hand and notices they stop *'on two shell scars'*. There is another shift in tone as he moves from a poetic image to the **register** of news reportage. He recalls the historical significance of the damaged road and places his memory of it *'in '92'*. **Alliteration** is used in a phrase which recalls newspaper headlines, as the observer remembers that it was here *'Serb mortars massacred the breadshop queue'*. The reader is shocked by the **visceral** images and horrific violence that follows. The place where the young lovers meet was once filled with *'blood-dunked crusts'* and the *'broken dead'* in the aftermath of a mortar attack.

The lines that follow form a lengthy complex sentence of multiple clauses as the poem describes *'the holes made by the mortar'*. This leads into speculation about what *'the boy sees'* but the reader is very much reminded of the violence which created the holes in the street. It is the site of the 1992 *'massacre'*. The scars in the road are deep and filled with water after a rainy day. Still hope persists – **alliteration** is used to draw attention to how

*'...even the smallest clouds have cleared away,
Leaving the Sarajevo star-filled evening sky'*.

The reporter in the poet cannot help bitterly reflecting how such a clear night would be *'ideally bright and clear for bomber's eye'*.

There is a jarring juxtaposition as the writer notes the mundane and ugly setting of *'those two rain-full shell holes'* yet imagines the boy sees twinkling stars, *'fragments of the splintered Pleiades'*. The **lexical choice** of *'fragments'* and *'splintered'* reminds the reader once again this is a city torn apart by sectarian violence and genocide.

The young couple are indistinct – *'the dark boy-shape'* and the *'dark girl-shape'*. It is a simple picture of teenage romance as they leave *'to share one coffee in a candlelit café'*. The poet once again intrudes with harsh reality – the *'curfew'* is not parental but a national curfew designed to protect citizens from snipers and mortar attacks. The people have been starved and the *'AID flour-sacks'* have now been repurposed and *'refilled with sand'* to form barricades. Bleak imagery pervades the poem yet the reader is left with a glimmer of hope, as the teenagers continue to meet, kiss and hold hands in a city scarred by conflict.

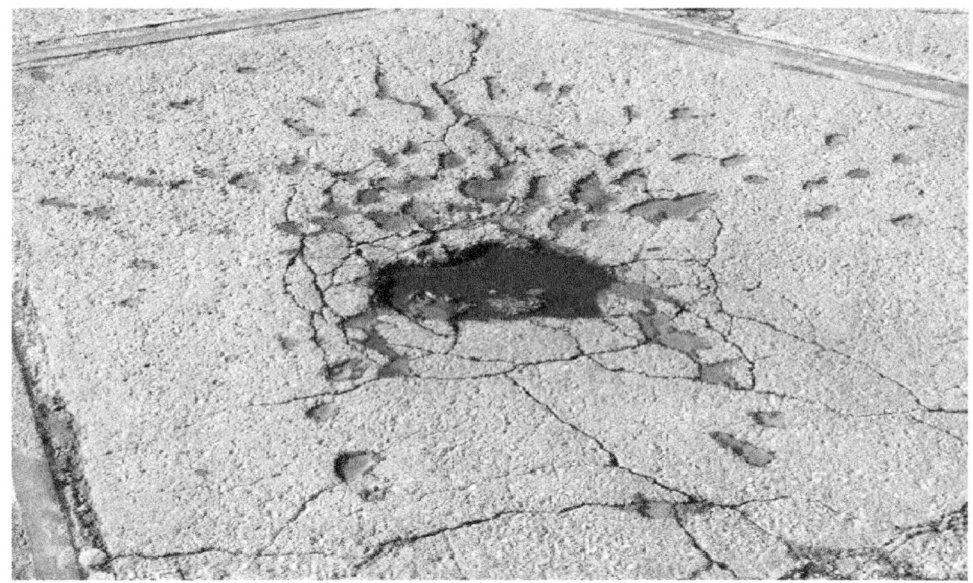

A 'Sarajevo Rose': damage caused by mortar shelling, painted red as a reminder of the lives lost.

1.7 *Disabled* by Wilfred Owen

This section will help you to;

- *Read and understand a variety of texts*
- *To selecting and interpret information, ideas and perspectives*
- *Understand and analyse how writers use linguistic and structural devices to achieve their effects.*

Disabled by Wilfred Owen - Background Context

The author, Wilfred Owen (1893–1918), is one of the best-known British poets of the First World War. He enlisted in the army in 1915 (aged 22) and fought in the Somme (in France) in the winter of that year. He was sent to Craiglochart Hospital, Edinburgh, to recover from shell shock, and wrote much of his poetry there. Although afterwards offered a home-based posting, he returned to the battlefield. He was awarded the Military Cross, then died a month later – a week before the end of the war. In hospital he would have seen many men like the one he described in this poem. The fact that the man may be Scottish (*'he'd look a god in kilts'*, line 25) is probably due to Owen's stay in a Scottish hospital. It is important to understand that the young man in the poem volunteered for the army. Conscription (compulsory service) was only introduced in 1916. However, even before this time there was some pressure on young men to enlist, some of it coming from women. (see line 26: *'to please his Meg'*). Around 800,000 British soldiers died in the war, and 1.6 million were wounded.

Content

This is a heart-rending poem in which a young man is observed ruminating on his current situation incarcerated in a hospital for injured soldiers and compares his dismal existence to life before the war when he was attractive, dynamic and admired

The poem, written in 1917, begins with a description of the disabled soldier sitting in his wheelchair. He has lost both his legs and most of at least one arm. He is full of mournful regrets. Initially he hears the boys, whose voices remind him of his own childhood, before he was wounded; then he remembers girls and thinks about how none of them will want him now. Even his face has grown old (stanza 3). He thinks of how he once liked to look heroic after a football match. This leads on to remembering the casual and rather vain reasons for his joining up.

We learn that he lied about his age in order to join up. This stanza also tells us that he hardly thought about the enemy or the reasons for the war. Rather, he looked forward to enjoying the glamorous image of being a soldier.

The penultimate stanza tells us that his welcome home was very different from his send-off. The poem ends with the young man anticipating a bleak future, pitied, and shunned by women. He is now almost completely dependent on others: he cannot even put himself to bed.

Task: Reading for Meaning: *Disabled*

1. Find the lines that show the following:

(a) He has no legs and possibly no lower arms.

(b) He will never again have his arm round a girl's waist.

(c) He used to like being thought of as a hero.

(d) He lied about his age and the recruiting officers probably guessed.

2. What were the young man's reasons for joining up and looking forward to a soldier's life?

Suggested Response to Task: *Disabled*- **Reading for Meaning**

1. Location of lines:
(a) His suit is *'Legless, sewn short at elbow'* (line 3)
(b) *'Now he will never feel again how slim/ Girls' waists are'* (lines 11–12)
(c) *'One time he liked a blood-smear down his leg,/ After the matches carried shoulder-high'*
(d) *'Smiling they wrote his lie'* (line 29)

2. He'd had a few drinks; someone said he'd look good in a kilt (worn by Scottish soldiers); and to please his girlfriend – who presumably thought he would come home safely.

He also looked forward to the smart uniform (*'jewelled hilts'* is a metaphor perhaps for parade dress; a hilt is the handle part of a sword); leave, the pay, and the sense of camaraderie (*Esprit de corps*).

Structure

The structure of the poem moves loosely from the present to the past, to the imagined future, and back to the chilly present, as the injured soldier waits powerlessly for someone to put him to bed.

Notice that the poem begins and ends with waiting. After the initial description, this structure follows the progression of the man's thoughts.

The poem is written in stanzas varying in number of lines, in iambic pentameter. There is a fairly regular rhyme scheme that makes the man's suffering slightly more bearable for the reader.

Task: Structure and Themes

The first stanza describes the man. Make up headings that sum up the content or themes of the remaining stanzas. For example, stanza 2 could be headed 'His regrets'.

Suggested Response to Task: Structure and Themes

Possible headings:
Stanza 1: *Alone;*
Stanza 2: *His regrets;*
Stanza 3: *Then and Now;*
Stanza 4: *Why he enlisted;*
Stanza 5: *Enlisting;*
Stanza 6: *Homecoming;*
Stanza 7: *Present and future.*

Style

The poem is in the **third person**, but the viewpoint is largely that of the young man. Hence the language is quite sparing, reflecting the man's bleak outlook and the fact that he is an ordinary young man, not a poet. There is little imagery and no elaborate use of adjectives.

However, there is slightly more of this kind of consciously poetic language in stanza 1, in which Owen is describing the man.

Task: Writer's Craft: *Disabled*

- What word describes the man's suit, and what is its effect?
- Stanza 1 contains a simile and a metaphor. What are they and what is their effect?
- Owen often uses irony in his poetry: appearing to say one thing but hinting at a different meaning. He does this in lines 10 and 17. Explain the irony and what it suggests.
- The poem ends with two questions, the second echoing the first. What do you think is their effect, and how satisfying do you find the ending?
- *'dark' (line 1)* means night, but what else could it also mean the man is waiting for, given his bleak prospects?

Suggested Response to Task: Writer's Craft

The suit is described as *'ghastly'*; this suggests that the suit is horrifying, more because of its being adapted to his injuries than because of its colour. Another meaning of *'ghastly'* is *'corpse-like'*. This suggests that the grey suit made him look like a corpse wrapped in grave clothes.

Simile: *'saddening like a hymn'* suggests that hearing the voices saddens the young man, because he thinks of his own childhood, when he had arms and legs; it also hints at disillusion with Christianity. It also suggests that some of the boys playing outside will also be lost in the war. **Metaphor**: *'Till gathering sleep had mothered them from him'* could mean that the boys' mothers have called them in; it also suggests that their absence soothes him.

Lines 10-17 are casual in tone, as if the man's terrible injuries do not matter. *'Throwing away'* his knees not only conveys the awful arbitrariness of war injuries, but also suggests that he was too casual in joining up: he threw away his youth and health in a thoughtless moment.
The phrase *'lost his colour'* means the blood has gone from his cheeks – normally just a sign that someone is under the weather.
This casual tone suggests that the man is thinking in a bitterly ironic way. (Perhaps Owen is as well).

The final questions suggest the uncertainty which now faces the man.

How will he survive, physically and emotionally? On the other hand, the repetition suggests the monotony that lies in store for him, always having to depend on others. They suggest that he has not yet come to terms with what has happened to him, and that he is emotionally very vulnerable.

It could mean that he is just waiting for death. At that time (1914- 1918), medical science did not offer wounded soldiers robotic limbs operated by small computers, nor could it even offer life-saving procedures that are available today. We need to remember that the kinds of injuries suffered by this soldier were treated under risky anaesthetics and, when healed, the disabled man would not be able to walk on wooden legs without lower arms to hold the crutches and sticks he would need to support him.

You should now read the detailed analysis to see how it compares with your response to the poem so far.

Further Analysis: *Disabled*

Stanza 1 lines 1-6

The seven stanzas are of irregular length. There is no regular rhyme scheme. The **third-person** perspective presents the unnamed '*He*'. The adjective title refers to this man '*sat in a wheeled chair*'. The use of the **gerund** '*waiting for dark*' suggests a sense of hopelessness and despair.

The **sibilance** in '*shivered in his ghastly suit of grey*'. The word 'ghastly' echoes 'ghostly' and conveys that he is lacking in life. The young man is known only as 'he'- while anonymous he represents every wounded soldier.

Owen shocks the reader with the word '*legless*'. It is a brutal truth. The young man is objectified as the poet describes his suit as '*sewn short at elbow*'. The reader is forced to picture his injuries. The young man's situation is contrasted with the boys playing. The **anaphora** of '*voices*' suggest they prey on his mind.

The use of **auditory imagery** as he hears the voices '*saddening like a hymn*'. This **simile** reinforces the idea of death-in-life, He perceives it as a funeral dirge.

The **alliteration** of '*play and pleasures*' highlight the contrast between their physical exertion and his inability to move. There are some examples of words rhyming within two or three lines of each other and within the stanza.

There is **personification** of gathering sleep. It has *'mothered'* him. This implies that his mother is not present. The modern reader might see this desire for sleep and night as a sign of depression.

Stanza 2 lines 7-13

There is a shift in **tone** as he remembers past joy, when lights *'used to swing so gay'*. The verse presents a swinging, happy scene. Inanimate objects seem to come to life. The lamps have *'budded'* and this metaphor makes this sound natural. There is a surreal image of the *'light blue trees'*. The condensed grammar is arresting as he recalls that *'girls glanced lovelier'*. The dash creates a break. It shatters the illusion and reminds him of his current loss. These are now *'the old times'*.

The **verb choice** is interesting. The poet suggests the man *'threw away his knees'*. The injury seems to be a waste and there is a suggestion it was a careless action. Owen here implies that becoming wounded in combat is not honourable but rather a foolish move.

The harsh truth remains that *'now he will never..'* The young man mourns the loss of physical contact. The use of the term *'girls'* indicates the man's youth to the reader. Owen chooses an unusual **adjective** when he describes the *'subtle hands'*. This presents a comparison between the delicacy of the girls' movements and the former soldier's brutal loss of limbs.

There is strength in the **simile** which presents the changing attitudes as the women now avoid him *'like some queer disease'.* They recoil from him. It provides a reflection of how he sees himself.

Stanza 3 lines 14-20

This stanza represents another shift in time. The poet reveals that the man was once considered physically attractive: *'There was an artist silly for his face'*.

The poem is structured by references to time, and changes in tense. These serve to provide a sharp contrast between the pleasures of his past life and the horrors of his abandonment.

Age is emphasised. He has a child-like face *'younger than his youth'*. This was only last year - *'Now, he is old'*. He feels he has lost his stature and strength, *'now his back will never brace'*. The reader must remember the young man is perhaps still a teenager.

There is bleak humour in the extension of the painting metaphor as it is remarked *'He's lost his colour'*. This is usually an idiomatic phrase used to describe when someone is feeling a bit ill yet here the meaning is brutal. The loss of colour refers to the severe loss of blood on the battle field.

The emphasis on visceral shock continues as the poet almost blames the boy on losing his own blood, as he *'poured it down shell holes'*. The use of **listing** and repeated 'and' while a *'lifetime lapsed'* indicates the sustained horror and pain. The dark image of the *'hot race'* as his blood raced to leave his body.

The one energetic image is the *'leap of purple'* which *'spurted from his thigh'*. There is **irony** in the dynamic choice of the verb *'spurted'* to describe a moment where his life is draining from him. It also reflects the poet's first-hand experience as it is an accurate way to describe the damage to an artery and the precision of the colour *'purple'*, which is a truer description of the appearance of blood, also suggests the poet has witnessed such injuries on the battlefield. This is one of the references to colour in the poem, providing an ironic contrast to the 'grey' of the first stanza.

Stanza 4 lines 21-28

This verse presents another memory as the boy recalls *'One time'*. There is bitter irony in the recollection that *'he liked a blood smear'*. The idea of masculinity when he was a teenager was linked to enduring sports injuries. He was idolised, *'carried shoulder high'* by his team.

The poet reveals the boy's motivation for joining up and volunteering for the war, suggesting he was drunk and confused;
*'...he'd drunk a peg/
He'd thought he'd better join. - He wonders why'*.

He demonstrates typical teenage vanity. He was tempted to sign up as a soldier because he was told *'he'd look a god in kilts'*. The young man does not confirm his reasoning. He does seem impressionable - he considers whether he was trying to attract a girlfriend. He joined *'maybe, too, to please his Meg'*. He confirms *'Aye, that was it'* and refers to the *'giddy jilts'*.

There is a turning point in the poem. There is a semi-colon suggesting a caesura in line 28 after *'He didn't have to beg;-'*. This shift in **tone** suggests the poet is about to reveal what he feels has been the motivating factor for the boy's situation.

Stanza 5 lines 29-36

This stanza provides a key piece of information, as the poet continues *'Smiling they wrote his lie; aged nineteen years'*.

This is the shocking truth of the poem and the target for the poet's anger. *'They'* are the officers who peddled propaganda. *'His lie'* relates to the fact that the boy was under-aged when he signed up for active duty. This would suggest that the broken and disabled man described in the poem may only be eighteen now.

The motivation of the young volunteer was not political. He seems unaware of the wider contexts as *'Germans he scarcely thought of'*. He joined as an act of bravado but went into battle with *'no fears/ Of Fear'*. Young soldiers are naive, intoxicated by the idea of uniform, pay and the *'esprit de corps'* of lads together. Owen is making a political point here, as he is critical of the ways in which young men were duped into going to war through nationalist propaganda.

Stanza 6 lines 37-39

This short stanza creates a **contrast** between the way the young men leaving for battle, who were *'drafted out with drums and cheers'* at the end of the previous line, and the isolation felt by the returning soldier who finds *'Some cheered him home, but not as crowds cheer Goal'*.

He has no support from the young women he once desired and pursued, *'only a solemn man'* who saw his shattered body and *'enquired about his soul'*. The older generation of men may well have participated in the Boer Wars and the question about soul hints at the psychological horror of war as the older man knows that the injured soldier's mind and spirit have been damaged.

Stanza 7 lines 40-47

There is a finality in the **adverbial** connective *'Now'*. The reader has been told he is a young man and are shocked when they discover he has *'a few sick years'* remaining. Families could not afford to care for physical injuries and these young adults were often abandoned.

There is a sharp **contrast** to the energy the boy had in his earlier life. He is now under the control of the nurses and must *'do what things the rules consider wise'*. He is passive and powerless, as indicated in the verb choice as he will *'take whatever pity they may dole'*. The young man sees himself through the women's eyes, as they *'passed from him to the strong men that were whole'*. They now see him as someone deficient, not quite human.

There is **rhetorical balance** in the return to the present as he realises it is *'cold and late'*. He has little to look forward to. The poet imagines the man's desperate thoughts - *'Why don't they come...'* He is thinking of the nurses but by extensions he misses his family, friends and Meg. The **repetition** of the question shows his desolation.

Structure

Owen links the narrative from verse to verse by **overlapping** rhyme patterns into new stanzas, for example *'grey'* and *'day'* in stanza one rhyme with *'gay'* in the second verse. The poem moves from a description of the young man sitting alone at the hospital to his past, carefree life to the horror of the injury on the battlefield and then back to the past. Towards the end we are taken back to the hospital and the final two haunting rhetorical questions that leave the reader, as well as the young man, contemplating his future.

The purpose of the poem is to convey his pity for his subject, the young man destroyed by war, and his anger against the authorities who encouraged the youth of each country to go to war. Owen also visits themes which are present in a number of his poems; the futility of war, the reality of survival, the loss of innocence and youth.

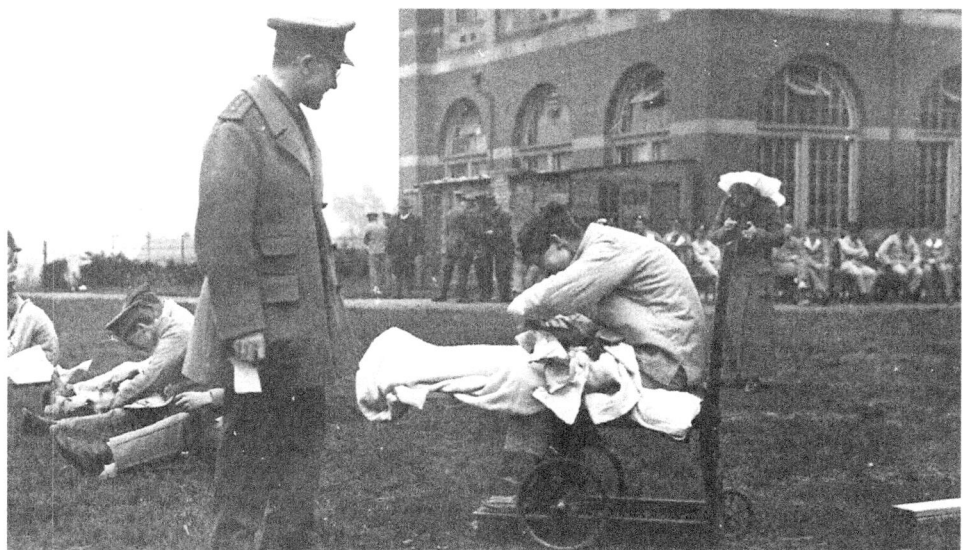

Injured soldier in chair

1.8 *An Unknown Girl* by Moniza Alvi

This section will help you to;

- Read and understand a variety of texts
- To selecting and interpret information, ideas and perspectives
- Understand and analyse how writers use linguistic and structural devices to achieve their effects.

An Unknown Girl: Background Context

Moniza Alvi is a Pakistani-British poet. She was born in Lahore in 1954 and moved to England as a child. She now lives in London. The narrator of the poem describes her visit to India and the time she had her hand hennaed with a peacock design by a girl in the market (the bazaar). The technique leaves a stain, rather like tattooing, but fades in a week or so (line 43). The narrator can be linked to Alvi herself, who openly expresses her longing for a deeper cultural understanding of Asia and her heritage in a number of texts.

Content

In narrative terms the poem's content is very simple: the poet goes to the market one evening and has her hand hennaed. She anticipates scraping off the dry henna to reveal the pattern staining her hand, which will fade in a week. She draws a link between the fading image and her fading connections with the culture around her.

Themes

Thematically, the poem is more complex. Possible themes to identify are:
- personal and cultural identity
- India and the West
- a sense of belonging
- loss and homesickness
- the familiar and the unknown
- memory

Task: Reading for Meaning: *An Unknown Girl*

1. What do you suppose it must be like for the poet to visit India, whose culture she feels is in many ways similar to that of Pakistan?

2. Which of the suggested themes do you feel are most reflected in the following lines?

(a) 'an unknown girl' (line 3, etc.)

(b) 'for a few rupees' (line 11)

(c) 'my shadow-stitched kameez' (line 15)

(d) '... Western perms./ Banners for Miss India 1993' (lines 22–3)

(e) 'people who cling/ to the sides of a train' (lines 34–5)

(f) 'When India appears and reappears' (line 44)

(g) 'longing for the unknown girl' (line 47)

3. Which theme(s) would you say were the most important in the poem, and why?

Suggested Response to Task: Reading for Meaning

1. The scenario that the poem presents must be quite a paradoxical experience for the speaker/ poet. On the one hand, India is in some ways a familiar culture, as the poet was born in neighbouring Pakistan; on the other hand she grew up in England and finds herself a tourist here.

2.
(a) personal and cultural identity; the familiar and the unknown
(b) India and the West
(c) personal and cultural identity; a sense of belonging
(d) India and the West
(e) loss and homesickness
(f) India and the West
(g) the familiar and the unknown; memory

3. You may have presented an opinion on which of the ideas or themes presented was most prominent in the poem. It is possible to argue that the wider concepts of personal and cultural identity are linked to sense of place, memory and belonging.

Analysis of *An Unknown Girl*

The poem is presented in one long stanza. There is no defined beginning or end. The poem presents a moment in time. The poet may be suggesting that India will always be beyond understanding or her mistakes may be repeated in other cultural settings. Another, more positive, perspective is that she will continue to try and develop her relationship with India and by extension seek to explore her family's roots in Pakistan.

The choice of **lexis** is culturally specific - words such as *'bazaar', 'hennaing'* and *'kameez'* suggest a tradition she wants to embrace. She is also introducing the reader to this world.

The phrase *'An unknown girl'* serves as a repeated **refrain**, appearing 3 times in the poem. The repetition of *'an unknown girl'* suggests layers of meaning. The girl is unknown in that she is a stranger but also suggests the speaker will never know what her life is like. The girl represents the mystery of India.

The specific art of henna-ing has cultural significance and the poet describes her response as she sits with the girl. The presentation of the short lines of the poem on the page may mimic the undulating lines of the henna tattoo. In line 7 she refers to the henna as *'icing'*. This reflects the decorative nature of the henna but also suggests it is an added beauty, not something that feels part of her.

In line 9 she makes reference to the artists *'satin-peach knee'*. It reflects her downy skin as well as suggesting a sensuous or exotic beauty. The use of the word *'satin'* connotes luxury.

There is repeated reference to the colours that surround her. There is a **contrast** provided which echoes the contrast between her English sensibilities and the brightness of India. The speaker is in local dress, a *'shadow stitched kameez'*, yet she seems detached from the scene in the *'evening bazaar'*.

There is use of **personification** in lines 17-21 as she reflects on the ways in which the *'colours leave'* and *'Dummies...tilt and stare'*, while the banners *'canopy me'*. She is an observer yet feels watched. In lines 22-23 the speaker seems almost disappointed by the Westernization of the girls around her, with the *'perms'* and posters for *'Miss India 1993'*.

The **syntax** reflects this as subordinate clauses build - she observes signs *'studded with neon'* (l.2). It seems brash in comparison to the way work is done *'deftly'*.

The speaker notes '*I have new brown veins*'. The image reflects the fine lines of the henna tattoo while suggesting there is a new cultural force running through her. The unknown girl is admired for her skill as she is '*very deftly*' creating the image of the peacock.

The henna tattoo appears larger and is described as peacock lines. It has captured her imagination and she is becoming entangled in the lines. The sibilance and assonance in the observation that the ink is '*soft as a snail trail*' conveys her curiosity.

The simile in lines 34-35 suggests the process is '*like people who cling/To the sides of a train*'. This is an image of desperation and recklessness which conveys the passion but perhaps the lack of commitment to the idea. She wants to cling to what she has. There is a degree of hyperbole here, as she compares her state of mind and desire to belong to those risking everything to make a journey to freedom or opportunity. Once again, the writer seems lost in a moment of self-reflection. Despite the bustle described earlier in the poem

'*Now the furious streets/
are hushed*'.

She does show pride in her '*new brown veins*' and feels more comfortable in her surroundings as the '*furious streets*' which were filled with bustle and energy are now '*hushed*'. There is a reverence and this experience of street art is elevated to a spiritual ceremony.

There is a shift to future tense as she considers how she will scrape off the dried henna and

'*reveal soft as a snail trail/
the amber bird beneath*'.

The speaker is referring to the henna art when she seems to sadly affirm that it will '*fade within a week*', yet the reader senses she is also referring to the fleeting nature of her experience on her visit. She is confident the trip will stay in her memory as she envisages an India that '*appears and reappears*'. Her sense of longing is confirmed with the lonely image of someone who will '*lean across a country*' to try and reach the unknown girl. For the speaker, this girl and this moment represent a culture she desires yet feels distant from.

As the henna is applied the speaker allows her mind to wander and considers how '*India appears and reappears*' in her mind and culturally. The '*amber bird*' suggests the ink is the colour of fire but also alludes to the phoenix and the idea of rebirth. There is an emphasis on colour and light throughout the poem which suggests the dynamic nature of the culture she has encountered.

Images of begging dominate as she imagines hands '*outstretched*', and speaks of '*longing for*' understanding. She has a desire to get close to this culture yet this girl remains '*unknown*'. Is this just a mystery or has she chosen to keep her distance?

Task: Writer's Craft - *An Unknown Girl*

The poem is very visual. Look at phrases like '*studded with neon*', '*icing my hand*', '*Colours leave the street*'. Which of these phrases are also metaphors?

Which one particularly relates to the theme of cultural identity, and why? (Clue: think of food!)

There is a lot to suggest colour in the poem. Pick out the lines that do this. What is the effect of including them?

The poet is attentive to small details, suggesting that the whole scene is wonderful, magical, to her and she is observing it all closely, perhaps hoping to fix it in her memory. Find three small, carefully observed details.

There is a powerful simile in lines 32–5. It relates to the fact that poor people in India often attempt to travel for free by clinging to the outside of the train.

The simile is appropriate in one way, in that the henna lines look something like railway lines, but in what other way is it appropriate?

In other words, how might the poet be clinging to the henna lines?

Structure

There is no rhyme or metre in the poem. However, two lines are used repeatedly.

What are they, and what is the effect in terms of the meaning and emotional impact of the poem?

Suggested Response to Task: Writer's Craft and Structure

'*Studded with neon*' and '*icing my hand*' are metaphors: neon lights are not actually studs; her hand is not actually being iced. This '*icing*' metaphor particularly relates to the speaker's own cultural identity because the henna marking being described is very much part of Indian culture, yet icing is what one does to an English cake, using a similar nozzle.

Neon lights are colourful; the henna is brown; *'peach'* is a colour as well as a fruit; *'Colours leave the street'*; a peacock, being drawn on her hand, is a very colourful bird; the brown henna will reveal *'an amber bird'*. The effect is to make India seem appealingly colourful, perhaps in implied contrast to England's greyness.

You may have chosen details such as *'which she steadies with hers/ on her satin-peach knee'*; *'As a little air catches/ my shadow-stitched kameez'*; *'Dummies in shop-fronts/ tilt and stare'*.

The speaker dwells on the image of people clinging to the train as it reflects how she might be clinging in the sense of clinging to her cultural identity, and how she will soon be clinging to her memories of India.

Structure

An Unknown Girl is written in free verse. The short lines could be read to reflect the bustle of the marketplace. There poem shifts from present tense to future tense at the end of the poem.

The narrator starts the poem in to the bazaar and informs the reader about what is happening. The setting is then described. The persona reflects upon the event in greater detail and then considers how this relates to her cultural identity and the long-lasting effect of her trip, returning in the last two lines to the girl and the bazaar. The poem repeats *'an unknown girl/ is hennaing my hand'*: these lines emphasise the strange and magical nature of the experience for the poet.

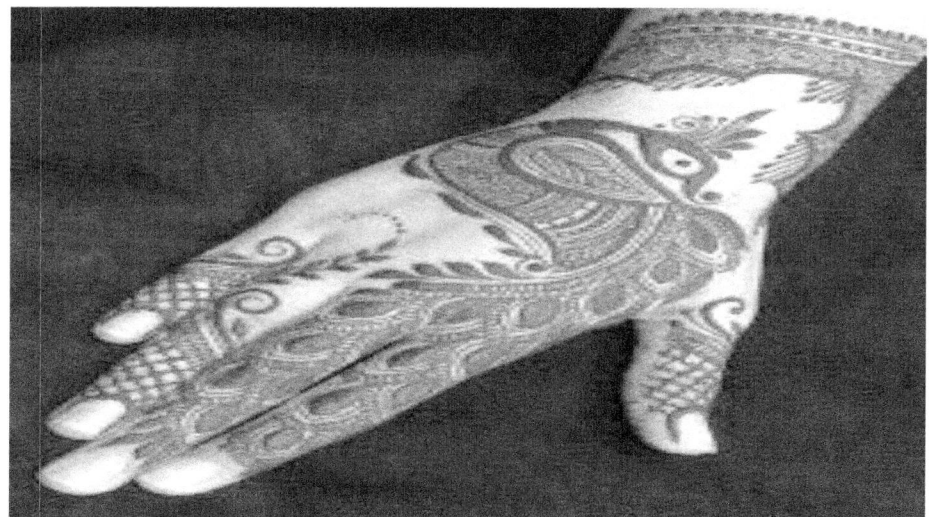

Henna artwork depicting a Peacock

1.9 *Out, Out-* by Robert Frost

This section will help you to;

- *Read and understand a variety of texts*
- *To selecting and interpret information, ideas and perspectives*
- *Understand and analyse how writers use linguistic and structural devices to achieve their effects.*

Out, Out- Robert Frost: Background Context

Robert Frost (1874–1963), was an American poet who lived for most of his life on a New England farm. He wrote this poem in 1915. It describes a real-life farmyard accident which had been reported in a local paper five years earlier. The poem is written loosely in **blank verse** (unrhymed iambic pentameter), which is the metre in which most of Shakespeare's plays are written. The title is a quotation from Shakespeare's *Macbeth*, in which Macbeth responds to news of his wife's suicide with a speech about the short and meaningless nature of human life. Part of the speech contains the line 'Out, out brief candle'. In this poem, the candle is a **metaphor** for life.

In the poem the phrase *'Out out, brief candle'* is a lament for a life cut short by accident or illness. The poet is lamenting the boy's sudden and arbitrary death. By alluding to Shakespeare, Frost is suggesting that there is tragedy in ordinary lives. 'Tragedy' here refers to serious dramatic tragedy as in *Macbeth*, or *Hamlet*, or Greek dramas such as *Antigone*. The title raises the boy's fatal accident from the level of ordinary, everyday life to one of heroic proportions. His death is like that of a Greek hero, an accident of fate.

Content

The poem is a simple narrative. A boy, probably a teenager, is using a chainsaw (buzz-saw) to cut wood for the family stove. A moment's inattention, probably caused by his sister announcing suppertime, leads to the boy losing his hand. To everyone's surprise, under ether anaesthetic, he dies.

Frost creates sympathy for the waste of a young life. The poem opens dramatically with the tool that will kill the boy. The object is presented in a sinister way before Frost relates the accident and its aftermath.

Task: Reading for Meaning: *Out, Out-*

1. It may be no accident that Frost wrote this poem during the First World War, when there was so much senseless loss of life. What do you find in the poem to suggest that the boy's death is similarly senseless?

2. What two lines describe the beautiful setting of the incident?

3. The word 'snarled', used in line 1 and twice in line 7 to describe the saw's sound, suggests that the saw has a life of its own. How does this hint at what is to come?

4. What other line suggests that the saw has a life of its own?

5. People often react strangely to shock. What seems strange about the boy's initial reaction?

6. Which lines suggest that the family did not care much about the boy? What do you think of this? Is there any possible explanation?

7. Why do you think the poet gave the poem a title that is a quotation from Shakespeare? What did he intend the title to convey to the reader?

Suggested Response to Task: Reading for Meaning

1. It is a random accident, injuring a boy who is perhaps too young to be using a chainsaw (*'big boy/ Doing a man's work'*). The boy's first response, oddly, is to laugh. The poem may be linked to the war in the senseless loss of young life.
2. *'Five mountain ranges one behind the other/ Under the sunset far into Vermont.'*
3. It sounds like a fierce animal (or a rattlesnake), which suggests a threat.
4. *'As if to prove saws knew what supper meant'* (line 15).
5. He laughs, probably not taking in the seriousness of the accident.
6. The end: *'And they, since they/ Were not the one dead, turned to their affairs.'* The explanation is unclear. Perhaps they have to work hard to survive, and throw themselves into work. Perhaps this is a way of escaping their loss. No mention is made of his sister's reaction.
7. The phrase *'Out out, brief candle'* compares a life cut short to an extinguished candle. By quoting Shakespeare Frost is suggesting that there is tragedy in ordinary lives. 'Tragedy' here refers to serious dramatic tragedy as in *Macbeth* or Greek drama, not the overworked use of 'tragedy' in celebrity gossip magazines, for example, 'tragedy as model trips up on the catwalk'.

Detailed Analysis of the poem

This 34-line poem is presented as free or blank verse. There is brevity in the title and a mystery which will be solved as the poem progresses. Some readers may recognise the allusion to Lady Macbeth in Shakespeare's *Macbeth* and realise that the poem may be referring to a life extinguished just as the 'brief candle' of Lady Macbeth's life is put out.

In line 1, the saw *'snarled and rattled'*. These aggressive verbs suggest the violence to follow. The saw is further **personified** in line 2 as it *'made dust and dropped stove-length sticks of wood'*. The **alliteration** and reference to the 'stove-length' cuts reinforced the power of the saw. This is juxtaposed with the feminine contrast of the sibilant description of wood as *'sweet-scented stuff'*.

The reference to *'lifted eyes'* places the reader in the yard and makes them part of the scene. The reference to specific features of the landscape emphasises the titanic nature of the natural features. The reference to a Vermont sunset places the poem in its American setting.

The **repetition** of harsh sounds in line 7 as the saw once again *'snarled and rattled'* creates a cacophony and conveys how the noise disrupts nature. There is syntactical balance as a contrast is made between *'light'* and *'load'* in line 8. The colon in line 9 creates a sense of status quo as *'nothing happened'*. There is a sense of resignation as the *'day was all but done'*.

The first-person voice presents the poet as a **witness** as in line 10 he reflects *'I wish they might have said'*. The desire in line 11 *'To please the boy'* presents this as both a memory of his own youth and an ominous foreshadowing of the horror to come.

It is clear the youth finds work a chore as in lines 11-12 hopes to be *'saved from work'*. This is a home with gendered sphere as his *'sister stood* 'and prepared *'supper'*.

In lines 14-15, the saw is once again given sentience and deemed malicious. What follows seems
'As if to prove saws knew what supper meant'.
Personification enacts the saw developing a life of its own as it *'leaped'*.

The pace of the poem is disrupted in line 17, as the narrative voice presents a reflection blessed with hindsight, ruminating on how *'he must have'*. This is interrupted with a savage moment of drama and horror as the observer struggles to convey the scene (*'But the hand...'*). The **repetition** of *'the boy'* in line 19 emphasises his youth and inexperience. The *'rueful laugh'* sounds sophisticated and resigned to fate.

The verb choice in line 20 as control is lost and he *'swung toward them'* emphasises the moment of realisation and despair as attempts are made to prevent *'life from spilling'* and *'Then the boy saw all-'* (line 22) as his fate becomes clear.

The use of **enjambment** across lines 23-24 remarks on the *'big boy/ Doing a man's work'*, creating a contrast between the dangerous job and the fact he was a *'child at heart'*. In line 25 the boy gains a devastating maturity as *'He saw all spoiled'*.

Dialogue is used in lines 25 and 26, with the dash and inverted syntax providing a heartfelt plea to his *'sister-'*. The tension of the **connective** *'So'* in line 27 is resolved with a quiet finality as he notes the boy *'was gone already'*.

Line 28 conveys the darkness of the unknown brought on by the *'dark of ether'* and the tragic exertion of the dying boy as he *'puffed his lips out'* (line 29). The dash and break in the line following *'And then-'* indicates the division between life and death. Line 30 concludes with a moment of alarm as he *'took fright'* before passing away.

The modified use of the past tense from line 31 emphasises how quickly the young man is consigned to history. The observer uses **dashes** both to convey the strength of his emotions and the brevity of existence as we become *'Little - less-nothing!'*. The boy's death evokes a reflection on the frailty of life and there is no optimistic look to an afterlife as the line ends with a **full stop** which indicates the end of all.

There is a grim irony in the **metaphor** in line 33 as the observer mourns the passing by realising there is *'No more to build on there'*. The boy had begun his day by building and constructing and now is dead. Wood has been cut and a life has been destroyed.

The use of **enjambment** in the closing lines reinforces the insignificance of our individual lives, as the narrative voice observes the reactions to the death. The others
*'..since they/
Were not the one dead, turned to their affairs'*.

The poem is **blank verse** with some use of iambic pentameter, although this is not consistent through the poem. Frost interrupts the regular meter to show that something has happened. The poetic flow of the poem is cut off, just as the boy's life will be cut short.

> **Other interpretations**
>
> Some critics argue that this poem demonstrates how work and tools force us into defined roles and regulate our lives. The poem is an indictment on the impact of mechanised labour.

Here, Frost writes from the perspective of a detached speaker. It is written as though a witness to the death, and this has some biographical context as Frost did see a young neighbour die in this way in his time cultivating his land.

As a **third person perspective**, the poem dwells on events and in many ways, tries to unravel the role of the saw or machine in what has happened.

Frost depicts changing moods effectively. He shifts from concern to seeming callousness when the boy dies. There is an emotional disconnect as the poetic voice presents its thesis - we work to avoid death - in terms of producing to gain shelter and sustenance - yet death is often cause by work.

There is a reserved silence. The reader shares the sense of loss and outrage with the witness.

In many ways this poem encapsulates a number of features known to be classic conventions of Frost's poems. He sets the scene in rural New Hampshire, near the Vermont border. The poem evokes an earlier traditional time. The family are using wood stoves to fend off the cold winter.

The buzz saw is described by sounds rather than visual imagery. It is animalistic - rather than fearing the wolf hiding in the undergrowth it now seems the danger is the encroaching industry in this rural setting.

Frost suggests this is a battle for the survival of human life - it is the machine against nature. He emphasises the struggle through contrasting enjambment and end-stops or dashes to suggest a disjointed experience destroying the harmony of nature. In the poem he jumps to the boy's voice. Throughout the earlier part there is the dull throb of the **alliteration** on 'd' with the aspiration on 'h' suggesting a breathless rush. The sound effects reinforce the description of events.

The **allusion** to the death of Lady Macbeth when she is mourned (*'Out,out, brief candle!'*) further suggests that the poem is concerned with the fragility and futility of life. Frost represents this fragility with his use of the dash to suggest a life cut short. The boy's bloody hand provides a visual echo to Lady Macbeth's attempts to clean the blood and guilt from her hands after murder. This may have been an analogy that came to Frost's mind when he witnessed the accident in reality.

Task: Style

The poem is written in **colloquial (matter-of-fact) language** – more or less the language of everyday speech. This is the style that Frost often wrote in, but it also reflects farm life.

What is the effect of the direct speech used in lines 14 and 25–6?

What phrases can you find which seem to echo everyday speech, in addition to the actual speech used?

Suggested Responses: Style

The **dialogue** makes the poem come alive, establishing a relationship between the boy and his sister. His appeal to her is pathetically moving. We are not told whether she was an older or younger sister, or whether they had parents to turn to. The boy's appeal to his sister suggests she may have cared for him as a younger sibling, but this isn't clearly stated. The *'They'* in the last lines of the poem may refer to the doctor and *'the watcher at his pulse'* (an assistant?), or to the people on the farm, or both. One possible reading is that the doctor and assistant left leaving the inhabitants on the farm to grieve; another is that the boy and his sister were working on a farm where nobody else cared much about them (the boy was made to work late). Another reading is that this was a household that accepted hardship with stoicism (without making a fuss), perhaps as part of a religious belief.

Many of the phrases are extremely plain, functional; e.g. '*As it ran light, or had to bear a load./ And nothing happened: day was all but done.*'; '*call it a day*'. *The boy gave his hand, as people do when they meet* (note the irony here); '*no more to build on there*'.

The poem returns to Frost's overarching theme about the brutality and force of nature. He admires it and desires to live a simple life, but his Nature is not sentimental and romantic - it is a landscape where people face misery and death. He conveys his difficult truth in a colloquial and simple language.

1.10 *Still I Rise* by Maya Angelou

This section will help you to;

- Read and understand a variety of texts
- To selecting and interpret information, ideas and perspectives
- Understand and analyse how writers use linguistic and structural devices to achieve their effects.

Still I Rise Maya by Maya Angelou: Background Context

Maya Angelou (1928-2014) was a successful African-American poet. First published in 1978, *Still I Rise* presents us with a strong black female narrator willing to speak up for herself, for other living black women, and for her black ancestors.

Still I Rise Language Analysis

Stanza 1

The opening stanza describes how the oppressors of black women have distorted views and peddle lies. She feels that her history has not been presented fairly, suggesting it is *'bitter, twisted lies'*. The speaker stresses the importance of a collective voice to make a presence felt.

Stanza 2

This section is presented as a pair of questions. It suggests the joys of the oppressor in constricting others, *'Sassiness'* reclaims a word used in a prejudicial way, suggesting that she has spirit and strength. The reference to *'Oil wells'* contrasts her values with capitalist society. Her wealth is her energy. Angelou faced many hardships in her own life and had to undertake a series of odd jobs and found herself in prostitution.

Stanza 3

The poem shifts to **future tense**. She will continue to rise. She is a force of nature- like tides and movement of the sun and the moon.

Stanza 4

Here she presents expectations. These men wish her to lower eyes and bow down. She will not submit.

The poem is in the second person and clearly addresses *'you'*. It is a bold, challenging address. She speaks for herself, ancestors and other women. The poem is political and personal. She refers to repression in literature. This transfers to writing, a move from domination to liberation. We must challenge thinking.

Line 3 refers to how others *'trod me'*. This is physical violence but also a lack of respect. The image of dust is pertinent as it is resilient and strong. It has a biblical allusion as we come from dust. This suggests the timelessness of the struggle.

Task: Individual Response

The above analysis comments on the first four stanzas of the poem. Read the remainder of the poem and try to trace the following features.

You should write up as notes, presenting at least two pieces of textual evidence (quotes) for each feature:

Poetic techniques:

- *Use of similes and metaphors*
- *Rhetorical questions*
- *Colloquial Language*
- *Personal pronouns*

Themes:

- *Pride*
- *Hope*
- *Endurance*

Suggested Response to Task: Individual Response

This activity required you to produce a detailed set of notes reflecting your own interpretation of the poem. There is no 'correct' response but the examiner will be assessing your ability to support your viewpoint with evidence from the text and discussion of the effects of the writer's choices. Here is an example of how you might choose to respond to one particular image:

This task required you to continue the detailed analysis of the rest of Angelou's poem. There are some details relating to structural patterns provided in this section. Here is a worked example of how to respond to language. The focus is an image from the final stanza. The speaker asserts:

I'm a black ocean, leaping and wide

The colour black can be presented with negative connotations, creating an ominous sense of fear and evil. It is an unusual adjective to link to the colour of water and evokes storms and a cruel sea which may harm those in it and on it. She is this ocean, which suggests the harrowing things which have shaped her. The use of black can also be linked to race- society likes to polarise into *'black'* and *'white'*. Here she sets the challenge that she is someone to be feared. She also has energy and limitless power, as she is *'leaping and wide'*. Like the sea, she will endure long after those who have tormented her have gone.

The writer's use of language

Similes used throughout the poem suggest that the speaker is a force of nature and will form a collective to illuminate the truth *'like moons and like suns'*.

The poem is built on comparisons and describes how she continues to lift herself emotionally and psychologically despite hardships faced. Her strength is conveyed through the use of anaphora as she continually asserts *'I rise'*.

The poem questions and challenges the reader and encourages them to empathise with how she has been made to feel. The **metaphors** employed celebrate her physicality as a treasure, in herself she has riches equal to *'oil wells'*, *'gold mines'* and *'diamonds'*. These things have connotations of luxury and are highly valued. The images are used to suggest that she values herself. She deserves respect and love more than these material things.

There is a degree of complexity with this reading, as while the speaker lists things which relate to material wealth, oil, gold and diamonds are also examples of the earth's resources which have been exploited. In this image she asserts her worth while subverting images of exploitation, although this may be a demand for acknowledgement, as historical slavery was an atrocious example of those in power exploiting other human beings.

The poem presents moments of great sorrow and degradation. The simile employed as the speaker pictures women with '*shoulders falling down like teardrops*' condenses centuries of physical and mental oppression. Dropped shoulders can imply a loss of confidence, physical exhaustion and emotional struggles. Here the image represents both her personal challenges and the fight against sexism and racism faced by black women through history.

She is not afraid to reclaim her sexuality, often regarded as a negative aspect of racial and gender stereotyping and challenges the reader to imagine the '*meeting of my thighs*'. She is no longer ashamed and refers to this part of her body as containing diamonds.

Black is used in the poem as a colour of celebration and is vivid. While other writers have used it to denote or connote fear or dread here the use is unexpected and powerful. It demonstrates how cultural conditioning imposes readings and highlights how wide the gap is to be crossed if we seek true equality and celebration of our differences. The poet addresses the readers and challenges them to reconsider their preconceptions.

The poem values humour - she celebrates that she has a '*laugh like gold mines*'. This **sensory image** conveys both the depth and quality of her laugh. Her treasure will be her ability to confront her enemies and rise above them.

Written in 1978 the poem also resonated with feminists. Although primarily about race it can address others who suffer discrimination and feel victimised. The message is that you must have pride and hope in self.

The poem does make clear reference to historical abuse and slavery. **Alliteration** is used to emphasise the fact that slavery has created a '*past of pain*'. There is an ironic reference to the '*gifts of ancestors*'. Generations of suffering have produced the strong and confident woman that she is today. The poem is written in the present tense. She has overcome hardships. She advises the reader to combat oppression with pride and grace. There is the image of air and dust rising. The emphasis on '*still*' suggests she will remain. There is a defiance and a sense of sisterhood. She continues to '*rise*'. She will grow and prosper, and invites the reader to do the same.

Structure

The poem has a regular structure of seven stanzas. Each has four lines with a regular *abcb* rhyme scheme. There is a dramatic shift in the second half of the poem. It could be regarded as a 15-line crescendo, with four rhyming couplets alternating with the repetition of '*I rise*' seven times.

There is a constant contrast with the violent actions and her bold response. The images are luxurious suggesting her worth. The tone is assertive. The history is painful but the speaker is not afraid to question her oppressors.

Maya Angelou

Photograph of Manderley

PART TWO Paper 2 Section B: Imaginative Writing

3.1 Personal Writing: Narrative Perspective
3.2 Imaginative Writing: Setting and Plot
3.3 Imagined Experiences: Developing Dialogue
3.4 Developing Narrative
3.5 Writer's Toolkit and Sample Assessment

PART TWO: IMAGINATIVE WRITING- links to exam

Part Two topics are all designed to assist in preparing you to complete the following exam paper component;

Paper 2: Section B Imaginative Writing

Section B: Imaginative Writing:

One writing task from a choice provided. Total for Section B: 30 marks.

You will be expected to:

- Use knowledge of wider reading to inform and improve your own writing
- Write effectively and coherently using the appropriate register, vocabulary, grammar and linguistic conventions

2.1 Personal Writing: Narrative Perspective and Figurative Language

This section will help you to;

- *Consider the skills required for imaginative writing*
- *Identify and use figurative language*
- *Discuss autobiographical writing, and write in this way yourself*
- *Understand and appreciate choices made in language, structure and form*
- *Communicate effectively, adapting form, tone and register of writing for specific purposes and audiences*
- *Write clearly, using a range of vocabulary and sentence structures*
- *Use appropriate paragraphing and accurate spelling, grammar and punctuation.*

Writing to explore, imagine and entertain

Paper 2 Section B is the Imaginative Writing element of the IGCSE qualifications. Essentially, this section will be testing your ability to write to **explore, imagine and entertain**. This will be the focus of the final module.

When you **explore**, you need to examine closely so may involve thinking about your thoughts or feelings about an experience or event.

Imaginative writing in this context means the creation of ideas or narratives.

Writing to **entertain** means that you hold the interest of the reader and this might be through enjoyment of a story. You may be asked to write about a favourite or memorable experience

Writing About Yourself

Why do we tell stories about ourselves?

Here are three pairs of possible reasons:

- to understand ourselves better
- to make a permanent record of our experiences
- to entertain people
- to help people know us better

- to earn money (through publication)
- to pass examinations

Task: Writing about yourself

What are the differences between the three pairs of reasons?

Jot down a few notes explaining the difference.

Suggested Answer to Activity

The first pair of reasons is *personal*. For instance, we might write a diary and hope that nobody else would ever read it (or perhaps we secretly hope that they will!).

The second pair of reasons is *social*. To put it another way, they are aspects of communication and they might help us build up friendships or keep our family amused.

The third pair is *practical*. We hope to gain something by telling a story well. That may be the most important one to you at the moment, if you are trying to pass an English examination.

But these different reasons often overlap and in every case we want to tell a story *well*. In this module of the course, we will concentrate on each of these different reasons, starting with the personal. This might mean writing about our own personal experiences and feelings or it might mean putting ourselves in someone else's shoes.

But what makes a good story about ourselves?

In Paper 2 Section B you may be asked to write a specific piece for a target audience. In one of the creative writing choices you may be asked to respond to a theme or element from the prose or poetry texts or a related image. You may be asked to describe an experience or event, either real or imagined.

Look at the following summary of events taking place in Europe in May 1940. This information has been taken from a history book on the Second World War:

May 10 1940 Holland, Belgium and Luxembourg invaded by German forces. Parachute troops landed near Rotterdam. British troops cross the Belgian border. Rotterdam bombed.

May 11 National (all-party) Government in England formed under Churchill.

May 13 Queen Wilhelmina arrives in London.

May 14 Rotterdam captured. Holland ceases fighting.

May 27 - June 4 Evacuation of British army from Dunkirk. It was four years, almost to the day, before they would return to liberate the occupied countries

---

Task: Personal Writing: Diaries

Imagine you are a teenager living in Rotterdam in May 1940 and you are filling in your diary as the days go by for the week beginning May 9. You are writing solely for personal reasons.

Try to invent suitable diary entries which express your hopes and fears as you watch the world changing around you.

Suggested Response to Task: Personal Writing

This was a personal writing task which was not being assessed. The aim of the activity was to encourage you to present a persona and imagined experience. You were able to imagine your life in Holland and how this was disrupted by the arrival of soldiers to your town or village. You might have included a description of your first impressions as the soldiers entered the town, or made a record of imagined interactions and thoughts and feelings about how your life may be about to change. You may have included a description of the bombing and to what extent you were affected by it.

The summary from the history book was brief and factual - in the diary task you were able to imagine a range of scenarios and create your own perspective.

Writing a Diary

Did you find it hard to put yourself in another person's shoes? In your dictionary, look up the word 'empathy'. This was an exercise in empathy — one of the skills you may be required to show in your examination.

It is probably easier to tell a powerful story if you are writing from your own experience.

Here are some extracts from Anne Frank's diary, detailing the change in circumstances for the Jewish community in occupied Amsterdam. The Frank family were eventually discovered and transported to Auschwitz on August 4th 1944:

> **October 20th 1942**: 'My hands still shaking, though it's been two hours since we had the scare... The office staff stupidly forgot to warn us that the carpenter, or whatever he's called, was coming to fill the extinguishers... After working for about fifteen minutes, he laid his hammer and some other tools on our bookcase (or so we thought!) and banged on our door. We turned white with fear. Had he heard something after all and did he now want to check out this mysterious looking bookcase? It seemed so, since he kept knocking, pulling, pushing and jerking on it. I was so scared I nearly fainted at the thought of this total stranger managing to discover our wonderful hiding place...'
>
> **November 19th 1942**: 'Mr. Dussel has told us much about the outside world we've missed for so long. He had sad news. Countless friends and acquaintances have been taken off to a dreadful fate. Night after night, green and gray military vehicles cruise the streets. They knock on every door, asking whether any Jews live there. If so, the whole family is immediately taken away. If not, they proceed to the next house. It's impossible to escape their clutches unless you go into hiding. They often go around with lists, knocking only on those doors where they know there's a big haul to be made. They frequently offer a bounty, so much per head. It's like the slave hunts of

> the olden days... I feel wicked sleeping in a warm bed, while somewhere out there my dearest friends are dropping from exhaustion or being knocked to the ground. I get frightened myself when I think of close friends who are now at the mercy of the cruelest monsters ever to stalk the earth. And all because they're Jews.'
>
> **May 18th 1943**: 'All college students are being asked to sign an official statement to the effect that they 'sympathize with the Germans and approve of the New Order.' Eighty percent have decided to obey the dictates of their conscience, but the penalty will be severe. Any student refusing to sign will be sent to a German labor camp.'
>
> Source: www. http://alphahistory.com/holocaust/anne-frank-diary-1942-44/

Although originally written for 'personal' reasons (Anne Frank had no idea her diary would one day be read by millions), it gives us a strong and detailed picture of what it was like to live through a comparable situation.

Task: First Person Perspective

Read the following passage, from *Heart of Darkness* by Joseph Conrad. In this extract, a character called Marlow is describing his fascination with exploration. In what ways does this piece of writing differ from a diary?

Now when I was a little chap I had a passion for maps. I would look for hours at South America, or Africa, or Australia, and lose myself in all the glories of exploration. At that time there were many blank spaces on the earth, and when I saw one that looked particularly inviting on a map (but they all look that) I would put my finger on it and say, 'When I grow up I will go there'. The North Pole was one of these places, I remember.
Well, I haven't been there yet, and shall not try now. The glamour's off. Other places were scattered about the Equator, and in every sort of latitude all over the two hemispheres. I have been in some of them, and ... well, we won't talk about that.

But there was one yet – the biggest, the most blank, so to speak – that I had a hankering after. True, by this time it was not a blank space any more. It had got filled since my boyhood with rivers and lakes and names. It had ceased to be a blank space of delightful mystery – a white patch for a boy to dream gloriously over. It had become a
place of darkness. But there was one river especially, a mighty big river, that you could see on the map, resembling an immense snake uncoiled, with its head in the sea, its body at rest curving afar over a vast country, and its tail lost in the depths of the land. And as I looked at the map of it in a shop window, it fascinated me as a snake would a bird – a silly little bird.

Suggested Response: First Person Perspective

The passage is similar to a diary in that it tries to capture the thoughts and feelings of a person at a particular moment in time.

But the most important difference is that it is written with hindsight (looking back over a period of years).

The writer creates a contrast between the adult Marlow who is speaking, and the boy Marlow he is describing. The 'I' in the sentence ' *'When I grow up I will go there'* ' refers to the child, while the 'I' in *'Well, I haven't been there yet, and shall not try now'* is the adult.

The first paragraph is an attempt by Marlow to capture his thoughts and feelings as a boy. Looking back over a gap of many years, we can say that this is a successful exercise in empathy because it is almost as if he was talking about another person.

The following section of the section involves a series of practical activities to help you prepare for guided imaginative writing tasks.

Imaginative Writing: Exploring and Creating Fiction

Fiction can be described as any kind of text that is not factual and it often takes the form of a story to convey a viewpoint or to entertain. Forms of fiction include short stories, novels, screenplay and drama. There are many different forms of imaginative writing. In the paper 2 examination, you will most likely be producing a piece of prose fiction.

Realism or the concept of 'realistic fiction' refers to narratives that although possibly produced by imagination could realistically happen. They may even be written around actual events, people and places- the genre of historical fiction is very popular, with novels such as *Wolf Hall,* based on historical English politics, selling well.

This type of fiction aims to make the reader feel as though they are reading about something that is actually happening and therefore events are described in a realistic rather than fantastical way, which enables the reader to imagine they are part of the event or story. Often the reader empathises with the characters as the narrative unfolds.

Non-realistic or 'fantastical' fiction, sometimes categorised as 'Fantasy', is fiction in which the events could not possibly happen in real life, so this means that they are either supernatural, have an alternative historical content, or include technology that has not been or could not be developed. Examples of this type of fiction are *Alice in Wonderland, Harry Potter* and *Lord of the Rings.* Often this type of fiction sits between realism and myth.

These types of texts often draw on familiar relationships from the real world, but present them in surprising ways. A successful fantasy series is *Game of Thrones*, which 'suspends disbelief' in its inclusion of dragons and walking dead, but has some historical basis in the factional conflicts of the War of the Roses.

Crafting Fictional Texts

There are a number of key elements of fictional texts. These include:

- **Plot**: This is how the narrative is shaped. It is formed by whet characters say, do or think and it unites the underlying story, giving it order and action. Plots have structure, put simply a beginning, middle and end.

- **Exposition**: the initial set up of a fictional text. Here you set the scene for the action.

- **Rising action**: This describes the linear progress of the narrative from exposition to the climax. It can be used to build suspense, as you encountered in the extract from ***The Woman in Black***.

- **Climax**: This is presented near the end of the written narrative - this is used to move towards a clear outcome or reveal truths.

- **Falling action:** This structure is normally found in tragedy or short stories. This refers to the effects of the climax and its resolution - in a short story this can be a 'twist in the tale'.

- **Resolution:** This occurs after the climax and is the final resolution for characters. It can be positive, involving a wedding or a reunion or negative, leaving the protagonist alone.

- **Conflict:** This is a key element of creative fiction and normally centres on the protagonist so that the reader can become engaged with the text. The conflict may be between abstract forces such as good and evil.

- **Foreshadowing:** This is a literary technique which can be effective, as it provides clues for the reader as to what might happen later on in the text. It prepares your reader for certain events or outcomes.

- **Character:** This is a participant in the story. The main character is known as the protagonist, with the main challenger often known as an antagonist.

- **Setting:** This refers to the location and time in which the story is set.

- **Theme:** This is a central idea which creates unity within the story. It can provide a moral or a message, as in the Achebe story in Section A.

- **Style:** This broad term refers to how the story is written and interpreted, so for example can refer to lexical choice, dialogue and perspective.

The following section of the guide involves a series of practical activities to help you prepare for guided imaginative writing tasks. This will be done by asking you to examine and evaluate the narrative techniques other writers use. You can then use your understanding of how writers achieve certain effects to help you model and improve your own creative writing.

Task: Planning Autobiographical Writing

You are going to write a passage of autobiography using techniques similar to those used in the passage from *Heart of Darkness*. You must be prepared to spend up to a few hours on this piece of work. However, it will be very rewarding, and will develop your English skills greatly.

In preparation draw up a short chronology of your life in diagram form:
Date...
Born in...
Sister born...
Started school ....

Include events of personal importance to you such as your earliest childhood memory, accidents, journeys, holidays, starting school, making a friend or an enemy, a death, a row, getting a pet, leaving home, leaving school, a sporting event, a personal achievement, and so on. Keep this chronology for use in subsequent writing activities.

Suggested Response to Task: Planning Autobiographical Writing

This activity required you to organise information from your own history and consider which events may be regarded as significant. Each of these events can form the focus for a short piece of autobiographical writing or be seen as a turning point or significant moment in your own development.

Task: Drafting Autobiographical Writing

Choose *one* of the events listed on your personal timeline in the previous activity. Your aim is to write about it in a way that describes it very closely. Only *after* you have given details of this event should you *then* describe the background to the event.

For example, information about time, place, the circumstances in which you were living, and the events that led up to this particular event.

Use the following scheme to organise your writing:

• **First paragraph:** Describe the event in detail, saying exactly what happened, and trying to give a picture of it.

• **Second paragraph:** Describe what sort of day it was and what recent events had led up to this event.

• **Third paragraph:** Give the date and your age. Describe what sort of person you think you were at the time.

• **Fourth paragraph:** Describe how you felt about the event at the time.

• **Fifth paragraph:** Describe how you feel now, looking back on the event.

General Notes:

• Write in the first person ('I', 'me', etc)

• Aim for approximately 500 words

• Write a rough draft, then re–write it.

Your aim is to **narrate**, that is, tell the story of an event, but to base the sequence of your writing on a movement from a specific event to explanations and discussions which provide a background.

This piece of work should not take longer than **45 minutes**.

Suggested Response to Task: Drafting Autobiographical Writing

These activities required you to organise information from your own history and consider how you could employ particular language techniques to entertain your reader.

The aim of the next activity is to change the point of view from which a piece of writing is told, so that you become aware of what differences this can make.

Task: Narrative Perspective

• Re–write the passage from *Heart of Darkness*, trying to keep everything the same, but writing in the third person, which means changing 'I' and 'me' to 'he' and 'his'.

• Now without looking at your own piece of autobiographical writing, write your own first paragraph again, describing the same event in your life, but writing a third person narrative. So that you write about yourself not as 'I' and 'me' but as 'she'/'her' or 'he'/'him'.

• Compare your two pieces of writing. Do you prefer your first person narrative or your third person narrative? Why?

Changing the Viewpoint

In writing about yourself as 'she' or 'he', you are making a greater difference between the person who tells the story, and the person the story is about. The teller is the **narrator** of the story. Even when you write as 'I', a first person narrative, there is a distance between the narrator (you telling the story) and the person who is experiencing events (you in the past). Most stories have a distinct narrator who tells the story and a principal character who experiences things.

Another way of putting this is to say that events are focused through a principal character, who is the 'focaliser'. So, in the passage from *Heart of Darkness*, for instance, the relationship is as follows:

Function: Narrator: The adult Marlow

Focaliser: The boy Marlow

Figurative Language

Figurative Language is language which creates special effects. You examined its use in your study of the anthology texts in earlier modules. This section will provide a review of elements of figurative language, as you will be expected to use some of these features in your own writing.

Similes

Here is a typical example of a simile: *'He sat in the corner as quiet as a mouse'*. In this phrase, the man's silence is compared to a that of a mouse, not because he resembles a mouse, but because both make very little noise. The special emphasis is on quietness. This is an example of a **simile**, one kind of figurative language.

In a simile, one thing is compared to another, from a different area of experience. The word 'like' often joins together the two sides of a simile. To make your writing interesting you should try to make unusual comparisons which create vivid images in the reader's mind, such *'he played the piano like a tap-dancing hippopotamus'*. We can imagine the noise and lack of grace of a large animal like a hippo and assume that the pianist is pounding the keys heavily with his hands. The idea of a hippo dancing adds a level of surreal humour to the image.

Metaphors

Metaphors also compare one thing with another. But here the connecting word is missed out altogether. Here are some examples: *'Murray's forehand went up a couple of gears in the second set'*; *'The pay was peanuts'*; *'That con artist really took me for a ride'*.

In the first case, the tennis player's performance is compared to that of a car or some other machine. In the second example, we understand not that peanuts changed hands but that the pay was not high enough. We might think of a small pile of nuts given to a large animal in a zoo. In the third, we understand that the con artist obtained the person's money in a devious manner. The metaphor is more abstract here as the idea of being taken along somewhere to distract you has become accepted as a short hand for being tricked or deceived.

The last two of these are examples of 'dead' metaphors because they have been used so frequently that we no longer see a picture of the object or idea that is being mentioned, e.g. the peanuts.

Task: Figurative Language: Similes and Metaphors

Can you find an example of a simile or metaphor in the earlier passage from *Heart of Darkness?*

Suggested Answer to Activity

An obvious example of an extended simile is: *a mighty big river, that you could see on the map, resembling an immense snake uncoiled, with its head in the sea, its body at rest curving afar over a vast country, and its tail lost in the depths of the land.*

At first this looks like a metaphor as it does not use the word 'like' or 'as' but the word 'resembling' provides the analogy.

The river is compared to a snake because of the way that it looks on the map. The mouth of the river looks like the head of the snake, and the river narrows towards its source as a snake narrows towards its tail.

There are four other techniques that writers use that you need to be familiar with, although some of them are more closely associated with poetry. These techniques can also be used in prose, so we have included a short description of them below, and some prose examples for you to consider:

Personification

When an inanimate thing is described as if it were animate, or is given human/animal attributes or qualities. In the example below, a mass of air is described as a 'tongue' which licks the 'crawling' ice to melt it. The ice is also described as 'decaying' like a dead body when in fact it is simply melting.

During the night a warm fluke, a tongue of balmy air, licked out from the mainland and tempered the crawling ice margins. The November snow decayed.

Annie Proulx, The Shipping News

Repetition

When the same words or phrases are repeated in one piece of writing, for narrative or poetic emphasis. Here Dickens is commenting on a particular age, or moment, in history. The repetition stresses the scope of the narrator's viewpoint:

> *It was the best of times; it was the worst of times.*
> *It was the age of wisdom; it was the age of foolishness.*

Charles Dickens, A Tale of Two Cities

Alliteration

When words placed close together in a sentence, line or paragraph start with the same sounds or groups of sounds. The next extract has repeated 'f' and 's' sounds, perhaps to imitate the sound of the water.

The Minke whale rose, glided under the milky surface... Again it appeared, sighed, slipped under. Roiling fog arms flew fifty feet above the sea.

Annie Proulx, The Shipping News

Assonance

When words placed close together have similar internal or vowel sounds. This is often difficult to spot. The extract above has some repeated vowel sounds – can you spot them? Collectively, these techniques are known as figures of speech or **figurative language**.

Writing About Yourself

Re-read your own autobiographical writing. Have *you* used figurative language? Have you compared anything with something else to create a special emphasis to show how something looked or to describe how you felt?

In your 3rd and 4th paragraphs, where you describe yourself and your feelings, could you have used figurative language to explain and describe things more clearly or powerfully? For instance, *'I felt as though a door had closed on my face.'* Or, *'I was like a ship adrift in an open sea.'*

Task: Using Figurative Language

- Write three sentences that describe you using figurative (comparative) language.

- Write three sentences that describe your feelings using figurative (comparative) language.

Note:

It should be possible to put these sentences into your autobiographical writing, to give it special kinds of emphasis, but do not rewrite your work. Add those sentences on a separate sheet.

This activity asked you to create 3 figurative sentences describing yourself which could be integrated into your autobiographical response. Some examples of describing feelings have been given in this section, such as *'I felt as though a door had closed on my face'* and *'I was like a ship adrift in an open sea.'*

Summary

In this section we have looked closely at personal, autobiographical writing or narrative, and have aimed to begin to develop your own writing skills in this area. We have also looked at how the specific meaning of a piece of writing depends on:

- the sequence of its parts

- its use of figurative language.

Now You Try It!

Write about a time when you, or someone you know, were tested to the limit.

Your response could be real or imagined.

2.2 Imaginative Writing: Setting and Plot

This section will help you to;

- *Consider the skills required for imaginative writing*
- *Explore different types of writing or narrative about personal experience, paying attention to their tone and structure*
- *Write imaginative and entertaining personal texts personal response*
- *Show an understanding of the devices and structures used by writers*

Ways of Telling

This section fits into the sequence on personal and imaginative writing, and continues the work of the previous section. It emphasises the different ways one may choose to describe events in the story.

Crafting a story or narrative

Narratives can take many forms. These can be short stories or full-length novels; individual books, trilogies (a story in 3 parts, such as *The Hunger Games*) or multi-volume series.

Professional writers have argued that short stories can be harder to write than full-length novels. As a student preparing for an examination which may ask you to write a short narrative under timed conditions, it is worth considering why this might be the case.

As for types of stories, which is also referred to as genre, an examination of a bookshop reveals a range of categories, including Science-Fiction, Detective or Crime Fiction, Mystery, Adventure, Supernatural and Horror Stories, Romances, Historical Fiction and Fantasy.

Not all narratives, particularly not all short stories, follow the same pattern. While we used a simple definition of narrative in the previous section, short narratives do not always have a beginning, a middle and an end in the traditional sense. In this section you will examine how many of the more successful stories will plunge you straight into the middle of the action while others will suspend you on a 'cliff-hanger', wondering what will happen next.

All stories do have at least three common elements:

1. **They have a setting**
2. **They have a plot**
3. **They have one, two or more characters**

---

1. They have a setting

This is the time and place when and where the story happens. It may be modern, historical or futuristic; it may be realistic or fantastic.

To convey a historical setting successfully, you need to know the period you are writing about extremely well. In an examination setting, there will be some degree of leniency with this, as original ideas will be awarded. However, given the challenges of crafting a creative text in timed conditions, It is best either to stick to what you know, if you are writing it is often best to develop a response with a recognisable setting; or to develop a narrative in a futuristic 'Sci-Fi' setting or a fantastical context.

---

2. They have a plot

This is the outline of the story - what happens, and the events that take place. Plots can be very simple or complicated.

For IGCSE, as you will be writing a relatively short response in the time available, it is best to keep your plot simple if you choose the narrative option.

---

3. They have one, two or more characters

These are the people concerned, the ones to whom the events of the plot happen. In short stories, it is best to keep the number of characters to a minimum. If you are writing anything other than fantasy or humour (both can be difficult in timed conditions), it is best to use realistic, believable names and outlines for your characters.

Task: Exploring the Writer's Craft: Route for Reading

When you have finished reading the passage overleaf, ask yourself the following questions in the following 'Route for Reading'.

What kind of text is it?

The Meaning of Words in the Passage

- Are there any noticeable features or problems of language?

- Are there any difficult words, ideas or sentences?

- Does the passage require specialised knowledge?

- Is the vocabulary or style unusual?

- Does the text contain all the information necessary for you to understand or respond to the passage?

The Organisation of the Passage

- How is the passage organised?

- How many sections are there, and how are they distinguished?

- How are these sections linked?

- If the sections of the passage describe a sequence of events, do they correspond to the sequence of the events in time?

Attitude

- Does the writer assume an attitude on the part of the reader?

- Does the writer present something as if it were fact?

- Does the writer take things for granted?

- Does the writer express any personal opinions as if they were fact?

What is its purpose? Who is its audience?

- What can I tell about the writer's context?

> *One evening of late summer, before the nineteenth century had reached one-third of its span, a young man and woman, the latter carrying a child, were approaching the large village of Weydon-Priors, in Upper Wessex, on foot. They were plainly but not ill clad, though the thick hoar of dust which had accumulated on their shoes and garments from an obviously long journey lent a disadvantageous shabbiness to their appearance just now...*
>
> *What was really peculiar, however, in this couple's progress, and would have attracted the attention of any casual observer otherwise disposed to overlook them, was the perfect silence they preserved. They walked side by side in such a way as to suggest afar off the low, easy, confidential chat of people full of reciprocity; but on closer view it could be discerned that the man was reading, or pretending to read, a ballad sheet which he kept before his eyes with some difficulty by the hand that was passed through the basket strap. Whether this apparent cause was the real cause, or whether it was an assumed one to escape an intercourse that was irksome to him, nobody but himself could have said precisely; but his taciturnity was unbroken, and the woman enjoyed no society whatever from his presence. Virtually she walked the highway alone, save for the child she bore...*

Suggested Response to Task: Exploring the Writer's Craft

The activity invited a personal response, but you may have made the following observations:

1. Kind of Text

It is a piece of fiction. The writer sets the scene, by describing the time and place and the characters so vividly, and with such precise detail, that it is hard to imagine that it could be a piece of factual description, or historical writing.

Although the scene is so realistic that one might think that it was an eye-witness account, the other features of the writing, discussed below, should have made you fairly sure it was a piece of fictional writing or narrative.

2. Language

Some of the vocabulary is slightly old-fashioned, implying that the novel was written some time ago (*'span... clad... hoar... intercourse...'*).

Some of the sentences are rather long and involved in their working through of the ideas or points of description involved. For instance:

> *They were plainly but not ill clad, though the thick hoar of dust which had accumulated on their shoes and garments from an obviously long journey lent a disadvantageous shabbiness to their appearance just now...*

In answer to the last question of this section of the 'Route for Reading', the writer does withhold information from us. As was said above, we are curious about the couple, who are merely described from the outside.

3. Organisation

The passage begins with a view of the couple from a distance, as in the use of an opening 'long shot' in a film. We see the couple and the large village they are approaching. Then we see their general aspect – the dustiness and shabbiness of their clothes. In the second paragraph, to the end of the extract, we are given a close-up view of the clothes, facial features and expressions, and behaviour of the couple.

The book works like a piece of cinema, selecting its angles and shots for effect and exploring the outside appearances of what is described, without giving definite information about the story and people involved – their histories or inner feelings.

4. Attitude

The writer makes us curious about these people by describing them as an onlooker would. The detail of the imagined scene implies a very great interest and involvement on his part in the story that is unfolding.

5. Purpose

The main purpose of the writing appears to have two aims. Firstly, the writer puts the scene vividly before us, and secondly the writer begins to get us interested in the characters described. As we read the passage, various questions about the identity, status, personality and relationships of the characters go through our minds.

It will come as no surprise, then, for you to learn that the piece of writing is, if you have not already come across the text before, a piece of fiction. It is from Thomas Hardy's novel, *The Mayor of Casterbridge*, and describes the progress of Michael Henchard, and his wife and child, to the village where the most fateful incident of their lives will occur.

Getting Started

The hardest part of crafting a narrative can be getting started. The opening needs careful consideration, as it has to 'hook' the reader, exciting their curiosity and engaging their interest in the development of characters and interactions.

One approach which can engage readers in an effective way is to begin the narrative *'in media res'* (in the middle of things). By placing the reader in the midst of an action, tension and suspense is created as there is interest in finding out more and making sense of words and behaviours.

Another arresting approach is to use direct address with a first-person narrator. This is when the protagonist speaks directly to the reader, inviting them to consider a scenario or reflect upon their own views. This can be presented as a question which requires immediate involvement in the narrative.

Another way to incite interest is to open the narrative with dialogue, placing the reader within a dramatic moment. As with *'in media res'*, the reader is then encouraged to read on to discover the wider context. Now read the extended opening extract from *Rebecca* by Daphne Du Maurier:

Last night I dreamt I went to Manderley again. It seemed to me I stood by the iron gate leading to the drive, and for a while I could not enter, for the way was barred to me. There was a padlock and a chain up on the gate. I called in my dream to the lodgekeeper, and had no answer, and peering closer through the rusted spokes of the gate I saw that the lodge was uninhabited.

No smoke came from the chimney, and the little lattice windows gaped forlorn. Then, like all dreamers, I was possessed of a sudden supernatural power and passed like a spirit through the barrier before me. The drive wound away in front of me, twisting and turning as it had always done, but as I advanced I was aware that a change had come upon it; it was narrow and unkept, not the drive that we had known.

The drive was a ribbon now, a thread of its former self, with gravel surface gone, and choked with grass and moss. The trees had thrown out low branches, making an impediment to progress; the gnarled roots looked like skeleton claws. Scattered here and again amongst this jungle growth I would recognise shrubs that had been landmarks in our time, things of culture and grace, hydrangeas whose blue heads had been famous. No hand had checked their progress, and they had gone native now, rearing to monster height without a bloom, black and ugly as the nameless parasites that grew beside them.7

On and on, now east now west, wound the poor thread that once had been our drive. Sometimes I thought it lost, but it appeared again, beneath a fallen tree perhaps, or struggling on the other side of a muddied ditch created by the winter rains. I had not thought the way so long. Surely the miles had multiplied, even as the trees had done, and this path led but to a labyrinth, some choked wilderness, and not to the house at all. I came upon it suddenly; the approach masked by the unnatural growth of a vast shrub that spread in all directions, and I stood, my heart thumping in my breast, the strange prick of tears behind my eyes.

There was Manderley, our Manderley, secretive and silent as it had always been, the grey stone shining in the moonlight of my dream, the mullioned windows reflecting the green lawns and the terrace. Time could not wreck the perfect symmetry of those walls, nor the site itself, a jewel in the hollow of a hand.

The terrace sloped to the lawns, and the lawns stretched to the sea, and turning I could see the sheet of silver placid under the moon, like a lake undisturbed by wind or storm. No waves would come to ruffle this dream water, and no bulk of cloud, wind– driven from the west, obscure the clarity of this pale sky. I turned again to the house, and though it stood inviolate, untouched, as though we ourselves had left but yesterday, I saw that the gardens had obeyed the jungle law, even as the woods had done. The rhododendrons stood fifty feet high, twisted and entwined with bracken, and they had entered into alien marriage with a host of nameless shrubs, poor, bastard things that clung about their roots as though conscious of their spurious origin. A lilac had mated with a copper beech, and to bind them yet more closely to one another the malevolent ivy, always an enemy to grace, had thrown her tendrils about the pair and made them prisoners. Ivy held prior place in this lost garden, the long strands crept across the lawns, and soon would encroach upon the house itself. There was another plant too, some half–breed from the woods, whose seed had been scattered long ago beneath the trees and then forgotten, and now, marching in unison with the ivy, thrust its ugly form like a giant rhubarb towards the soft grass where the daffodils had blown.

Moonlight can play odd tricks upon the fancy, even upon a dreamer's fancy. As I stood there, hushed and still, I could swear that the house was not an empty shell but lived and breathed as it had lived before.

Light came from the windows, the curtains blew softly in the night air, and there, in the library, the door would stand half open as we had left it, with my handkerchief on the table beside the bowl of autumn roses.

The room would bear witness to our presence. The little heap of library books marked ready to return, and the discarded copy of The Times. Ash–trays, with the stub of a cigarette; cushions, with the imprint of our heads upon them, lolling in the chairs; the charred embers of our log fire still smouldering against the morning. And Jasper, dear Jasper, with his soulful eyes and great, sagging jowl, would be stretched upon the floor, his tail a–thump when he heard his master's footsteps.

A cloud, hitherto unseen, came upon the moon, and hovered and instant like a dark hand before a face. The illusion went with it, and the lights in the windows were extinguished. I looked upon a desolate shell, soulless at last, unhaunted, with no whisper of the past about its staring walls.

Task: Imaginative Writing - Further Exploration

When you have read the passage, answer the following questions:

- Consider how the paragraphs are ordered. Is this a 'linear' narrative in which a straightforward time–sequence is followed, or is time rearranged in some way?

- Considering the tone of the passage, is it detached and objective, or is it emotional and imaginative?

- What information are we invited to seek for between the lines about the former life of the dreamer and the former state of the house?

- What information would we wish for about events, and the identities of the people involved?

Suggested Response to Task: Imaginative Writing - Further Exploration

In answering the exploratory questions, we might wish to explain;

- why the house is apparently deserted;
- why the narrator might dream about returning there;
- who the narrator is, whether a man or a woman, and whether old or young;
- who is the master of the house; and
- whether the past referred to was a happy time or not.

In the first four paragraphs, the movement of the speaker is along the drive to the house.

From paragraph 5 and 10, the dreamer's journey continues, even though she does not get any closer to the house. You should try to explain the journey that takes place in her mind, with reference to each paragraph in order, starting at paragraph 5.

Paragraph 5: She stands looking at the house from outside.

Paragraph 6: She turns to look towards the sea and then turns back to the house, and sees the garden round it in more detail.

Paragraph 7: She begins to travel back in time, seeing the house as it was before the time of her dream.

Paragraphs 8 & 9: She has gone back in time in her mind and focuses on the windows. In her imagination, she sees the inside of the room.

Paragraph 10: She realises she is still outside the house, and back in the present of the dream.

The reader sees everything through the eyes of the dreamer, so the route you describe is also an account of the viewpoint offered to the reader. This is an emotional, imaginative viewpoint, not detached, objective or rational. The dreamer cannot tell the difference between fantasy and reality, and there are many things about this house and its past that we are not told.

Organising Narrative: Plot

The **plot** is a specific order that the writer has chosen to arrange events in the story or poem. A plot is not necessarily chronological but a story is the chronological order in which the events would have occurred. This distinction is useful. Plots help us understand facts and gather knowledge about what we are reading, for example readers must be given information about certain aspects early on and other aspects can be concealed until later. This process can be used to develop tension.

Places and locations form what we refer to as the **setting** of a narrative. Settings often stick in our minds when reading any piece and therefore this is an important aspect of any fictional writing. The setting may make us think of a personal experience; somewhere we have been or just trigger our imagination to create an image in our minds as we are reading. Settings can also create mood and also help the characterisation and dialogue that may be included.

Manderley, the house in the dream, is described in a number of ways because of the dreamer's mixed emotions about it, and because its former glory contrasts so strongly with its present decayed state.

Crafting Descriptive Writing: Adjectives

Descriptive writing puts into words what a person, thing or place is like. Good descriptive writing should make the object, place or person being described come alive in the reader's imagination. Descriptive tasks require you to produced detailed writing that creates vivid images in the reader's imagination.

As you progress through the GCSE course, you will develop your selection and use of adjectives in your creative and functional writing.

Adjectives are words used to describe a noun. They are chosen by writers to add description and mood to a piece of writing in particular ways.

For example, consider the difference between the sentences '*I fell into the river*' and '*I fell into the raging river*'. The adjective '*raging*' adds description to the sentence. It helps the reader get a clear picture of what is being described. The reader can now imagine the scene vividly: a rapidly flowing river. The adjective also adds tension to the sentence and wider narrative. The word '*raging*' makes the river sound fast flowing and dangerous. This makes the sentence more exciting for the reader, who anticipates a threat to the narrator.

When deciding to add detail to your writing through the addition of adjectives, make sure to use a word which makes <u>sense</u> in the sentence. Sometimes the use of an overly formal word or a word which is from a different historical context can have a jarring and disruptive effect.

EXAM TIP

When considering adjectives and other ways of demonstrating lexical skill, always ask yourself if you have introduced better vocabulary to your work. It can be better to keep your style sparse than use bland or childish-sounding adjectives such as '*big*', '*nice*', '*interesting*', or '*scary*'.

When adding detail to your work, aim to use an adjective that creates a specific image or particular mood for the reader. Manderley, the house in the dream, is described in a number of ways because of the dreamer's mixed emotions about it, and because its former glory contrasts so strongly with its present decayed state

---

Task Improving Imaginative Writing 2: Adjectives, nouns and verbs

From the list of adjective nouns and verbs listed below, select those which:
(a) indicate what the house was like in the past
(b) indicate how empty and deserted the house is now
(c) indicate how the dreamer has preserved the memory of the house in her mind.

secretive	desolate	shell
tired	tomb	untouched
permanent	breathed	symmetry
silent	unhaunted	light
shining	sepulchre	jewel
ruin	soulless	inviolate

Task Imaginative Writing: Structure and Lexical Choices

Use the list of adjectives from the last activity to help you write a paragraph about the different states of the house. Re-read the passage to remind you, and use some adjectives of your own choosing. You should structure it like this.

'Manderley was once …

… Now the house is …

… However, in the mind of the dreamer it will always be…'

Suggested Response to Task: Improving Your Imaginative Writing

The activities build together to support you in the production of an extended imaginative response. A model response, an extract from the novel *Rebecca* using these words in context, is provided below:

> At first I was puzzled and did not understand, and it was only when I bent my head to avoid the low swinging branch of a tree that I realised what had happened. Nature had come into her own again and, little by little, in her stealthy, insidious way had encroached upon the drive with long, tenacious fingers. The woods, always a menace even in the past, had triumphed in the end. They crowded, dark and uncontrolled, to the borders of the drive. The beeches with white, naked limbs leant close to one another, their branches intermingled in a strange embrace, making a vault above my head like the archway of a church. And there were other trees as well, trees that I did not recognise, squat oaks and tortured elms that straggled cheek by jowl with the beeches, and had thrust themselves out of the quiet earth, along with monster shrubs and plants, none of which I remembered.
>
> Manderley was once a place of light in which people lived and breathed contentedly. Its design was perfectly symmetrical and its ideal setting made it like a jewel. Now the house is an empty, deserted ruin. It has been left desolate and soulless like a tomb or a dead body. However, in the mind of the dreamer it is still untouched and inviolate, for no-one can rob her of her memories. To her it is still a place which preserves silent secrets, and it will never be completely unhaunted while she keeps alive her memories.
>
> Although the real house decays, the dream house is permanent.

2.3 Imagined Experiences: Developing Dialogue

This section will help you to;

- *Consider the skills required for imaginative writing*
- *Distinguish between alternative forms of written English*
- *Communicate effectively, adapting form, tone and register of writing for specific purposes and audiences*
- *Write clearly, using a range of vocabulary and sentence structures*
- *Use appropriate paragraphing and accurate spelling, grammar and punctuation.*
- *Write convincingly about imaginary experiences*
- *Analyse a literary passage in some detail*
- *Present dialogue and find suitable speech patterns for different characters*

Introduction to Imagined Experiences

Paper 2 will include a choice of writing tasks to demonstrate your ability to explore, imagine and entertain. To make this writing come alive, you will need to write imaginatively, with detail that makes the experience seem real. We will be looking closely at such writing in this section and, hopefully, give you help with writing in this way yourself.

In previous sections we have looked at writing about an actual experience, and also about crafting an imagined experience, looking at the description, points of view, and personal feelings expressed.

For this section, you will be undertaking close analysis of a range of extracts from *Great Expectations* by Charles Dickens. These have been selected to provide models of specific literary techniques, such as **sensory description, irony, hyperbole** and characterisation through **dialogue.**

In this section, in looking again at an imaginative piece of writing, we will be giving you the opportunity to choose appropriate vocabulary to describe scenes and the characters' feelings. You will also practise writing dialogue and a letter, in order to be able to express personal reactions, and to use language appropriate to these forms of writing.

Imaginative Writing

The last section of the guide emphasised some of the different ways in which accounts of actual or imagined experience (what people feel and do) can be written. In this section we will look closely at a piece of writing which communicates a very vivid personal response, on the part of the character, to what he sees.

Pip arrives at Barnard's Inn (from Charles Dickens, *Great Expectations*, chapter 21)

We entered this haven through a wicket-gate, and were disgorged by an introductory passage into a melancholy little square that looked to me like a flat burying-ground. I thought it had the most dismal trees in it, and the most dismal sparrows, and the most dismal cats, and the most dismal houses (in number half a dozen or so), that I had ever seen. I thought the windows of the sets of chambers into which those houses were divided, were in every stage of dilapidated blind and curtain, crippled flower pot, cracked glass, dusty decay, and miserable makeshift; while To Let To Let To Let, glared at me from empty rooms, as if no new wretches ever came there, and the vengeance of the soul of Barnard were being slowly appeased by the gradual suicide of the present occupants and their unholy interment under the gravel...

Thus far my sense of sight; while dry rot and all the silent rots that rot in neglected roof and cellar — rot of rat and mouse and bug and coaching-stables near at hand besides — addressed themselves faintly to my sense of smell, and moaned, 'Try Barnard's Mixture'. So imperfect was this realisation of the first of my great expectations that I looked in dismay at Mr. Wemmick. 'Ah' said he, mistaking me; 'the retirement reminds you of the country. So it does me.'

Note: Dating back to the fourteenth century, Barnard's Inn was an inn of chancery in Holborn, London, where students studied law. By the nineteenth century it had become dilapidated and run down. No longer an inn of chancery, the rooms were let out as residential chambers (or studio flats as we would call them today).

Task: Responding to Literary Texts: Pip at Barnard's Inn

In the extract above, Pip describes his arrival at Barnard's Inn, a group of old buildings in the City of London. Try to analyse the passage you have read, and identify its purpose and its important features, in terms of writer's choices and how the reader may respond to these choices.

When you have done this, compare your answers with the suggested response.

Suggested Response to Task: Responding to Literary Texts

In your answer you might have mentioned that this passage is a piece of fictional narrative, in which a character narrates his experience in the first person. The piece contains specially chosen descriptive vocabulary such as *'disgorged'*, *'dilapidated'*, *'makeshift'* and *'interment'*. (Make sure you understand these words: if you do not, look them up in your dictionary). Dickens evokes both the sights and sounds experienced by Pip.

The main part of the text is the first long, descriptive paragraph. This is followed by a second short paragraph which introduces the beginning of a dialogue between Pip the narrator and Mr. Wemmick.

The attitude of the writer is one of aversion towards the scene described. The purpose of the text is to give the reader a vivid and imaginative impression of a scene. The writer is seeking to influence the reader to see the scene as unpleasant.

Setting

Choosing the right setting for your narrative is crucial. If you want to seize the reader's interest you must capture their imagination and make them care about the world you are describing enough to read on.

Setting can guide reader's expectations, particularly in genre-based writing. In crime, horror or mystery fiction, it can enhance your effectiveness if you select a setting which helps to create an apt mood.

It can increase tension and suspense if you place your character or narrator in an unfamiliar or threatening environment. If your protagonist is weak or vulnerable it will create empathy and engage the reader's curiosity.

Isolated locations also increase dramatic effectiveness as a character can be shown to be alone and unable to seek help easily and quickly if a problem should occur.

Wherever type of setting you choose for your imaginative response, you must describe it in vivid detail to make the place come alive in the reader's mind. To do this you should aim to describe the place in a multi-sensory way. Effective description appeals to all senses and conveys the character's emotions. Dickens has illustrated this in his reference to the sights and smells that greet Pip as he enters the Inn.

Task: Considering Writer's Techniques

In this activity you will complete a number of short tasks which ask you to identify and examine the effects of the writer's techniques of description:

- Barnard's Inn, where the passage is set, is initially described by Pip as a *'haven'*. Look up the word 'haven' in your dictionary, and explain with reference to the passage whether or not 'haven' is an appropriate word to describe Barnard's Inn.

Suggest why Pip used this word.

- The storyteller imagines the influence of the original Barnard, after whom Barnard's Inn is named, in two figures of speech.

The first is a simile, the second is a metaphor. In the case of a simile, a writer says something is like something else (e.g. 'he eats like a horse'; 'she looked as if she was stone'...); a metaphor is similar, but here a writer talks about something as if it were something else, without using words like 'like' 'as' and so on which make it obvious there is a comparison (e.g.: 'he is a horse when he eats; 'she turned to stone'...). The first figure of speech, the **simile**, likens Barnard's influence to that of his soul still haunting the premises.

The second figure of speech, the **metaphor**, refers to an imaginary 'Barnard's Mixture' as the cause of the smells and atmosphere of the Inn. Explain in a bit more detail and in your words, what effect the soul of Barnard is described as having on the tenants of Barnard's Inn.

Secondly, explain in your own words what real things Pip is describing as the imaginary 'Barnard's Mixture'.

Finally, be sure you grasp the difference between a metaphor and a simile.

Suggested Response to Task: Considering Writer's Techniques

'Haven' means a place of retreat, shelter or security. This is not an appropriate word to describe Barnard's Inn, because Pip finds the place unpleasant and even repellent so he would not choose it as a place to find shelter or security. In short, he would not like to live there. He calls it a haven in order to be *ironic*. He says what the place is not, but what he would have liked it to be.

Calling it a haven is an *ironic* way of pointing out the contrast between what he hoped for, and the disappointing reality

Irony

Irony is a figurative device in which a word, phrase or tone is used to mean its opposite. For instance, *'what lovely weather'* to describe bad weather. It is often conveyed by the tone of voice of the speaker. When analysing the writer's attitude, we need to consider whether he or she is being ironic about a person, place, event or outcome. The *'soul of Barnard'* is imagined to be taking revenge on, or having an evil influence on, the people who live in Barnard's Inn.

While the reality is that most people have moved away from the area, Pip imagines Barnard's ghost has driven them to suicide and that their bodies are buried under the gravel. In an extract rich in sensory description, Pip then imagines that the rotten smells which exist in Barnard's Inn are speaking to him with voices, as if they are a strong-smelling concoction or mixture, made by an imaginary Barnard.

Like the irony used in the choice of the word *'haven'*, these extended similes comparing real things (at least, real within the world of the novel) with imaginary things are ways of producing a very exaggerated or powerful description or emphasis. This figurative use of language is called **hyperbole**. It is not meant to be taken literally.

The activity that follows will enable you to explore the feelings of Pip, the narrator of the passage. You will be asked to present your understanding of why Pip reacts as he does to Barnard's Inn. Pip is being taken to Barnard's Inn by Mr Wemmick because he is going to live there.

Task: Narrative Perspective

Consider these questions, then write a paragraph in your own words, but supporting your statements from the passage. You should deal with these points:

- Has Pip visited this place before?

- Is he accustomed to big cities?

- How might he have been feeling just before he sees the place where he is going to live?

- The *'retirement'* (seclusion) of Barnard's Inn reminds Mr Wemmick of the countryside. Does Barnard's Inn remind Pip of the countryside?

Suggested Response to Task: Narrative Perspective

You can guess that Pip has not visited this place before because of the detail with which he describes the smells and sights as if they shock him, and he refers to what he 'thought' about the place, rather than what he knew. It seems that he is not accustomed to big cities, as he cannot imagine how the 'present occupants' of the place can bear to live there. The trees and animals seem miserable and pathetic to him, and he may be comparing them in his mind to the trees, birds and cats he has seen in the country. He also seems surprised at the cramped conditions in which people live, noticing that the houses are 'divided' into 'sets of chambers'. He refers to his 'great expectations', suggesting that he had high hopes, or anticipated something special.

He may have thought that his new residence would be much smarter and more prosperous in appearance. Mr Wemmick 'mistakes' him, or misunderstands his disappointed reaction. It seems likely that Pip finds this place very different from the country. Pip's own reaction is one of 'dismay'.

Narrative Perspective: First and Third Person Perspective

The two most familiar ways of presenting a story are to write from the First Person or the Third Person perspective.

First Person narrative is where all the action is seen through the eyes of the main character, and it is written as though he or she is writing. It resembles non-fiction texts, particularly autobiography. Pip in *Great Expectations* directly addresses the reader as he recounts the story of his life and 'expectations'.

As a writer, one advantage of using first person perspective is that it can feel easy and natural as a writer, and usually does not demand very complex grammar, although this is not always the case, as with the presentation of Pip, whose formal and convoluted syntax often reflects his own social aspirations.

The disadvantage of first-person narrative is that your reader can only know what your main character knows. If something happens somewhere where your character is not present, you cannot 'know' about it unless someone else in the story tells your character about it. In this way, it can be a restricted narrative.

Some writers use this potential limitation for particular effect, as with F Scott's Fitzgerald's *The Great Gatsby*, where the narrator's admiration of Gatsby's romantic outlook make him an unreliable and biased narrator of the events leading to Gatsby's death.

Third Person narrative is where the action is seen through the eyes of the storyteller. This persona is omniscient as they have a privileged view of events and are even able to comment on the thoughts and motivations of a range of characters.

The third-person or omniscient narrator presents events in a similar way to a television or film camera and the reader is given information on everything that is going on. There are practical advantages when using third-person perspective. The main character does not have to be involved in every interaction. The author and the reader can 'know' things that the main character does not know.

The passage you have read implies or suggests how Pip feels by showing how he sees the scene he describes, but it does not directly describe his feelings.

Task: Arresting Adjectives

This Task continues from the one you have just completed. It will help you to develop your insight into Pip's feelings and his personal experience. You are going to write about Pip's feelings before and after seeing Barnard's Inn for the first time. To help you do this, read through the following list of nouns taken from the passage, of the things he dislikes about the place:

- dilapidation
- decay
- dirt
- overcrowding

Then read through the following list of adjectives which he uses to describe what he doesn't like about the place:

crippled cracked dusty small dismal

miserable flat melancholy neglected

Go through the list of adjectives again, and for each one find an adjective which has an opposite meaning. For instance, for 'crippled' you might choose 'healthy', 'strong', 'vigorous' or 'sturdy'.

Write a paragraph from Pip's point of view, describing his feelings, using the first person, 'I'. You should describe first of all his feelings of anticipation/expectation before he sees Barnard's Inn.

The passage you have read *implies* or *suggests* how Pip feels by showing how he sees the scene he describes, but it does not directly describe his feelings.

Remember that he was brought up in the country and this is his first visit to the city. He is about to see the place where he is to live. You should then describe how he feels about the crowded city buildings. You should also say what sort of surroundings he was used to before. In your answer, make use of the adjectives you have listed, to describe what sort of environment Pip was used to.

Suggested Response to Task: Arresting Adjectives

This activity aims to support your writing as you develop your lexical choices. Your answer might have been along these lines:

As I approached the place where I was to live, I felt **anxious and excited**. I was expecting something **impressive / grand / awe-inspiring/ dignified / fashionable** as my new home. I was **optimistic and my hopes were high**. However, when I saw my future home I was **outraged** and felt as though I had been **deceived**. I had been used to **cheerful / spacious / hilly / open** surroundings. I had always lived in a **clean / fresh / cultivated /cared-for / healthy** place and I had not realised how **dismal and dingy** the city would be. I had imagined that it would be a **prosperous, comfortable and smart** place and I felt **disappointed / horrified / shattered / mortified / outraged / frustrated / cheated / utterly downcast** by the grim reality of Barnard's Inn. The **miserable** sights and the **decaying** smells that met me were completely **unexpected** and not at all what I had **anticipated**. I felt **repelled / depressed / sickened / put off / nauseated** within the first few seconds of my arrival, I was **determined** that I would not and could not stay there.

This suggested answer suggests a series of adjectives that you might have used in your answer. Re-read your own answer and improve it by inserting some of these adjectives into it to make it more fully descriptive of Pip's feelings.

When you have chosen the adjectives you think are most appropriate, and checked the list given in the answer to see if you can find any that are more suitable, write a sentence suggesting why the writer chooses to use the word 'dismal' four times in one sentence. What effect do you think he was trying to achieve?

Then write a sentence suggesting reasons for the use of the word 'rot(s)' four times in the following sentence:

'Thus far my sense of sight; while dry rot and all the silent rots that rot in neglected roof and cellar — rot of rat and mouse and bug and coaching stables near at hand besides — addressed themselves faintly to my sense of smell...'

Again, you should consider what effect the writer intended to have on his audience.

Task: Writer's Craft

In this activity you will examine the writer's use of repetition and choose adjectives appropriate for a particular effect.

'I thought it had the most dismal trees in it, and the most dismal sparrows, and the most dismal cats, and the most dismal houses (in number half a dozen or so), that I had ever seen.'

Try re-writing this sentence, substituting for 'dismal' four other adjectives that mean something similar. Try to fit the replacement adjective in each case to the object(s) it describes.

You could choose from the following list:

*gloomy miserable brooding unlucky dreary joyless
dull pathetic glum depressing unhappy
grim sorrowful mournful fateful unfortunate*

Suggested Response to Task: Writer's Craft

You have probably noticed that the writer uses long sentences, and that many of the sentences consist of a series of clauses linked by commas or by 'and'. For instance:

'I thought the windows of the sets of chambers into which those houses were divided, were in every stage of dilapidated blind and curtain, crippled flower pot, cracked glass, dusty decay and miserable makeshift...

There are a number of possible answers here, all of which might be true. For instance, the writer may be seeking to emphasise or **exaggerate** one thing by repeating a word over and over again; he may wish to make the word stick in our minds. However, he is also telling us about Pip's reaction to what he sees, and giving the impression that Pip is so disgusted that he is lost for words, and has to keep using the same words. The **repetition** is also intended to make the reader visualise or imagine the same quality over and over again, so that we have a feeling of the repetitive monotony, the lack of variety, in the scene that is being described.

You will read about some more types of repetition that occur in the passage, and consider their intended effect. To appreciate this effect, you will be asked to read the passage aloud to yourself.

To appreciate the dramatic effect of this writing, you should read the passage aloud allowing your voice to express more and more distaste as each sentence progresses. Start each sentence in an ordinary, calm way and put more feeling in your voice, building up to the end of the sentence. The writer of the passage, Charles Dickens, wrote his books to be read aloud to a listening audience. Reading it aloud will enable you to experience the dramatic potential of the passage.

The activities will help you to develop your appreciation of the dramatic intention and effect of this passage. This will also increase your understanding of the reactions, feelings, and points of view of the narrator, Pip. To appreciate the purpose and effect of this piece of writing, it is important to consider it as a story told to an actual audience. Pip tells the story of his childhood and youth in the novel *Great Expectations* by Charles Dickens.

Pip tells the story of his childhood and youth in the novel *Great Expectations* by Charles Dickens. The story is told in such a way as to teach many sections about life, and to warn listeners about Pip's mistakes. Therefore, the story has two purposes: to entertain and to instruct. It is helpful to imagine Pip telling his story to a young listener; this would explain why he uses the variety of figurative language and dramatic storytelling devices you have learnt about in the previous activities. He wants to keep his listener entertained, but he also wants to make his meaning very clear.

Note on Technical Accuracy: Presentation of Dialogue

When portraying the speech interactions between characters you should observe the rules of paragraphing and punctuation for dialogue.

Start a new line and paragraph for each speaker.

Insert **quotation marks** around direct speech.

Task: Transforming Texts: Creating Dialogue

Your task is to re-write the passage, transforming it from a piece of descriptive narrative to a dialogue between Pip and his listener, a child or a young person.

This is an example of how it could begin:

'What was it like, Uncle Pip, when you got there? Was it as good as you expected? Was it really grand? Was it a big house on the main street? How did you find it?'

'We entered this haven through a wicket gate, and were

disgorged by an introductory passage into a melancholy little square that looked to me like a flat burying-ground.'

'But what were the houses like? Weren't there any gardens with trees?'

'I thought it had the most dismal trees...'

Guidance on Task

You should observe the rules of paragraphing and punctuation for dialogue used here. Start a new line and paragraph for each speaker. Insert quotation marks around direct speech. Insert a question from the listener at the end of each sentence. You should show that the listener responds to what has just been said, and asks a question which is answered by the next sentence Pip speaks. The questioner is curious, involved in the story and wanting to know all about Pip's feelings and the events he describes. Pip is trying to do two things: he wants his listener to see the scene described as he saw it, and he wants the listener to understand his reaction to it.

The questions the listener asks should include questions about:

- The detailed appearance of the buildings

- Whether there were any people in Barnard's Inn

- The atmosphere of the place

- How Pip felt

- What Pip did

The listener should also react to what Pip says, for example:

'How awful...'

'It sounds horrible...'

'You must have been disappointed...'

When you have written this dialogue, read it through, and you will be able to see how Pip's story would affect a sympathetic audience. You will see that this writing is designed to produce a strong sympathetic reaction from its audience.

Task: Evaluating Dialogue

The following passage is a piece of conversation from the same novel, Great Expectations. In this activity you will use this passage to learn to identify points of view, characters and their reactions.

Read through the following 'conversation' carefully, several times, trying to work out how many people are speaking and when each character is speaking. You may use a number system in pencil alongside each piece of speech. So, put 1 against the first speaker, and 2 against the second, and identify who is speaking throughout.

'Hold your noise! Keep still, you little devil, or I'll cut your throat!'
'O! Don't cut my throat, sir. Pray don't do it, sir.'
'Tell us your name! Quickly!'
'Pip, sir.'
'Once more, give it mouth!'
'Pip. Pip, sir.'
'Show us where you live. Pint out the place!'
'You young dog, what fat cheeks you ha' got. Darn Me if I couldn't eat 'em, and if I han't half a mind to't!'
'Now lookee here! Where's your mother?'
'There, sir! Also Georgiana. That's my mother.'
'Oh! And is that your father alonger your mother?'
'Yes, sir, him too; late of this parish.'
'Ha! Who d'ye live with - supposin' you're kindly let to live, which I han't made up my mind about?'
'My sister, sir - Mrs. Joe Gargery - wife of Joe Gargery, the blacksmith, sir.'
'Blacksmith, eh? Now lookee here, the question being whether you're to be let to live. You know what a file is?'
'Yes, sir.'

> 'You know what wittles is?'
> 'Yes, sir.'
> 'You get me a file. And you get me wittles. You bring 'em both to me. Or I'll have your heart and liver out.'
> 'If you would kindly please to let me keep upright, sir, perhaps I shouldn't be sick, and perhaps I could attend more.'
> 'You bring me tomorrow morning early, that file and them wittles. You bring the lot to me, at that old Battery over yonder.
> You do it, and you never dare to say a word or dare to make a sign concerning your having seen such a person as me, or any person sumever, and you shall be let to live. You fail, or you go from my words in any partickler, no matter how small it is, and your heart and your liver shall be tore out, roasted and ate.
> Now, I ain't alone, as you may think I am. There's a young man hid with me, in comparison with which young man I am a Angel. That young man hears the words I speak. That young man has a secret way pecooliar to himself, of getting at a boy, and at his heart, and at his liver. It is in wain for a boy to attempt to hide himself from that young man. A boy may lock his door, may be warm in bed, may tuck himself up, may draw the clothes over his head, may think himself comfortable and safe, but that young man will softly creep and creep his way to him and tear him open. I am keeping that young man from harming you at the present moment, with great difficulty. I find it very hard to hold that young man off of your inside. Now, what do you say?'
> 'Say Lord strike you dead if you don't!'
> 'Now, you remember what you've undertook and you remember that young man, and you get home!'
> 'Goo—good night, sir.'
> 'Much of that! I wish I was a frog. Or a eel!'

Suggested Response to Task: Evaluating Dialogue

On close examination you will see that there are two people speaking. They usually speak in turn. Check through your numbering, so that next to line 1 you have indicated speaker 1, and next to line 2 you have indicated speaker 2. Line 3 is speaker 1 again, and so on.

You can distinguish between the two speakers in two main ways:

1. The way they speak: Speaker 2 uses standard English. Speaker 1 sometimes mispronounces words such as *'partickler'* for 'particular', and uses *'ain't'* instead of 'am not'.

2. The relationship between them: Speaker 1 asks the questions and threatens Speaker 2. Speaker 2 is clearly afraid of Speaker 1, and answers Speaker 1's questions, but is sometimes afraid to speak, for instance, between lines 8 and 11. Speaker 1 is the more powerful figure in this interaction.

Structuring Dialogue

Dialogue can be described as the engagement in words of one character with another – so one character speaks and the other replies. However, in some texts there may only be one speaking character – the overall inference will still be clear. The basic pattern of any dialogue is declaration and response – if you think about any conversation you have had today and analyse it you will see how this pans out. In some of the texts you have already studied dialogue reflects verbal mannerisms of speech and also class and dialect; these things give the text authenticity.

Direct and Indirect Speech

Direct speech is what a character says:

'John has accepted the position,' said Tim

'Oh that's good,' replied Sarah. 'I hoped he would.'

Tim glared at her and retorted, 'I think he has a cheek after all he put us through over the last few weeks. When I think of all the wasted evenings talking him through things, I can't get my head around it!'

'You invited him,' replied Sarah, giggling nervously.

Tim stormed out of the room and slammed the door.

The speech is enclosed in inverted commas with a single punctuation mark before they are closed around the text – normally a single comma unless it signifies the end of a sentence when a full stop would be used. Obviously question marks and exclamation marks can also be used.

It is customary to start a new paragraph at the beginning of the sentence which contains dialogue. When the dialogue has ended and the narrative resumed, a new paragraph is commenced.

Indirect or Reported Speech

Indirect speech does not use the exact words of a speaker but provides a summary of what they have said. It can be used to provide variety or to move the narrative on at a faster pace.

In the example above you might change the last example of Sarah's words to *Giggling, Sarah reminded Tim that he had invited John.*

Dialogue and the use of inverted commas or 'speech marks'

Inverted commas can also be used to identify direct quotations and titles, examples:

He went to see the film *'The Force Awakens'*.

In this instance, the full stop comes outside the inverted comma.

Direct Speech:

If a direct quotation comes within a section of dialogue, double inverted commas can be used so that it is easily identifiable.

'Matt is coming on Friday,' said Claire.

Indirect Speech

Claire said Matt would be coming on Friday.

Indirect speech does not need inverted commas.

Task: Characterisation

This activity gives you practice at describing characters. Look back at the extract of dialogue with the two unnamed speakers. For each of speakers 1 and 2, describe their:

- age;
- gender;
- social class;
- way of using language;
- occupation.

Support all your conclusions with evidence from the text.

Suggested Response to Task: Characterisation

Speaker 1:

Age and Gender:

Adult, male: Pip refers to the speaker as *'sir'* (line 3), and he must be older, since he regards Pip as young.

Social Class and Language Use:

You can deduce something about speaker 1's social class from the way he speaks. He pronounces 'point' as *'pint'* (line 8), 'particular' as *'partickler'* (line 34), and 'vain' as *'wain'* (line 41). He uses colloquial language such as *'ye'* for you (line 15), *'lookee here'* for 'look here', or literally, *'look you here'* (line 19), and 'to be let to live' for 'to be allowed to live' (line 20). There are many other examples that suggest speaker 1 has a regional accent and the fact that he speaks colloquially combines with the regional accent to suggest he comes from a working-class background.

Occupation:

All we can deduce is that speaker 1 is in hiding, as he tells Pip not to *'say a word'* (line 31) to anyone about having seen him, and to get him a file and some food (*'wittles'* = victuals). From this we can guess that he may be in trouble and hiding from the law.

Speaker 2:

Age and Gender:

Young, male: he is referred to as *'little devil'* (line 2), *'young dog'* (line 9), and his name is Pip. Later, when speaker 1 in trying to frighten him, he talks about what his friend will do to *'a boy'*. Speaker 2 is a boy.

Social Class:

Pip lives with his sister who is the wife of the blacksmith (line 18), so he belongs to the rural craftsman or artisan class.

Language Use:

Pip's use of language is polite and grammatically correct. He uses standard English.

Occupation:

As he is looked after by his sister and her husband, either he does not have an occupation, or he is the blacksmith's assistant.

Task: Setting and Plot

This Task asks you to describe the scene and what is happening:

• Try to work out where the two characters (Pip and the man) are. What are their immediate surroundings, what time of day is it, and what general area are they in?

• You should then describe this, supporting your description with evidence from the text.

• Next you should describe what you think is happening between the characters, again using evidence from the text to support what you say.

Suggested Response to Task: Setting and Plot

They are in a graveyard, where Pip points out to the man the graves of his parents, '*Also Georgiana*' his mother, and his father, '*late of this parish*'. The actual inscription on the gravestone is *'Philip Pirrip, late of this parish, and also Georgiana wife of the above.*' It is evening or night, as Pip wishes the man good night in line 53. They are probably out in the country, as no-one else is around. In line 54 the man says '*I wish I was a frog or a eel.*' From this we can deduce that they are in a wet place such as a marsh.

The man is threatening Pip with a knife (line 2), and is holding him.

In line 26, Pip asks him, '*let me keep upright*', so we can deduce that the man is holding Pip upside down, making him feel sick. The man makes Pip tell him who he is, where he lives, and with whom.

When he discovers that Pip lives with a blacksmith he tells him to get him a file and some food and bring them to him in his hiding place in the old battery (an old gun placement). He threatens Pip and tells him about a vicious '*young man*' hiding with him. He says this man will kill Pip if he dares tell anyone what has happened. Pip sets off, frightened, to do what he is told. We can tell he is frightened because he stammers '*Goo—good night*' in line 53.

Task: Dialogue and Characterisation

This task gives you more practice at writing dialogue. It also asks you to make use of the descriptions you have written of the characters and what is happening. The task is designed to teach you to explore reactions, and describe characters and a scene, using clear and well-selected detail, as well as to use language imaginatively.

In the extract from Great Expectations consisting of the dialogue between Pip and the man, only the direct speech has been presented to you.

Your task is to take the section from line 8 ('Show us where you live...') to line 28 ('...and perhaps I could attend more'), and fill in the descriptions of the actions and kinds of voices which would give a clearer picture of what is going on in the scene. Consider how the characters speak:

loudly timidly quietly fearfully

quickly powerfully threateningly

You should describe what they are doing as they speak. Here is an example, from the beginning of the passage:

> 'Hold your noise!' cried a terrible voice, as a man started up from among the graves at the side of the church porch. 'Keep still, you little devil, or I'll cut your throat!'
> A fearful man, all in coarse grey, with a great iron on his leg. A man with no hat, and with broken shoes, and with an old rag tied round his head. A man who had been soaked in water, and smothered in mud, and lamed by stones, and cut by flints, and stung by nettles, and torn by briars; who limped, and shivered, and glared and growled; and whose teeth chattered in his head as he seized me by the chin.
> 'O! Don't cut my throat, sir,' I pleaded in terror. 'Pray don't do it, sir.'
> 'Tell us your name!' said the man. 'Quickly!'
> 'Pip, sir.'
> 'Once more,' said the man, staring at me. 'Give it mouth!'
> 'Pip. Pip, sir.'

You will notice that the story is told in the first person by Pip, and you should continue this. Start a new line and paragraph for each speaker. Before the inverted commas close, you should punctuate with a comma, a full-stop, a question mark or an exclamation mark.

You should only use a comma before closing the inverted commas if a sentence of speech is being broken in the middle. If you break the speech to insert 'said...' or 'shouted...' you should always use a lower-case letter, not a capital letter. Speech must always be punctuated before the inverted commas are closed. If in doubt, look at examples in stories like this.

Characterisation

It is often characters rather than events that make stories memorable. One of the most exciting things about reading and creative writing is the opportunity it provides for readers and writers to imagine what it is like to be someone else, to identify with another character.

When we are reading a novel or other story, we identify with characters in the story either because they seem real to us or because they appeal to our dreams and fantasies.

The essential thing about any main character in a story is that he or she should be in some way interesting or intriguing. They must do and say things not just because that's the story, but because they have motives and reasons for doing and saying what they do.

The characters you put into your stories have got to be real to you, otherwise, they won't be real to your readers. This means you must have, in the back of your mind, some idea of every aspect of the lives your main characters at least, even if all we see of the characters is a small slice of their lives, a 'snapshot' taken from the whole.

Now You Try It!

Continue a story, which begins;

'He could resist everything except temptation, and this was very tempting ...'

2.4 Developing Narrative

This section will help you to;

- Consider the skills required for imaginative writing
- Distinguish between alternative forms of written English
- Communicate effectively, adapting form, tone and register of writing for specific purposes and audiences
- Write clearly, using a range of vocabulary and sentence structures
- Use appropriate paragraphing and accurate spelling, grammar and punctuation.
- Identify the features of factual and fictional reporting of experience
- Use a number of different formats and styles appropriate to different purposes and audiences
- Consider the ways in which a writer turns raw material into prose.

Introduction

This section continues the series on turning personal experience into imaginative prose. In this section you will be looking at a number of pieces of writing concerned with the experience of war. You will be identifying features of writing which gives a factual account and writing which gives an imaginative account.

Task: Real and Imagined Experience

Read through the extract below carefully. You should make notes on the following:

What kind of writing is this?

What is its purpose?

Are there any difficult words? Which ones, if any, are difficult, and why?

How is the writing organised?

What attitudes does the writing communicate?

> *Rain and sleet and sun, getting guns camouflaged, stealing a Decanville truck, laying out nightlines. Letters from Hodson, Eleanor and Sgt. Pellissier. Still that aching below the nape of my neck since my last O.P. day. Sat till 11 writing letters. As I was falling asleep great blasts shook the house and windows, whether from our own firing or enemy bursts near, I could not tell in my drowse, but I did not doubt my heart thumped so that if they had come closer together it might have stopped. Rubin and Smith dead tired after being up all the night before. Letters to Helen and Eleanor.*
>
> *28. Frosty and clear and some blackbirds singing at Agny Chateau in the quiet of exhausted battery, everyone just having breakfast at 9.30: all very still and clear: but these mornings always very misleading and disappearing so that one might almost think afterwards they were illusive. Planes humming. In high white cloud aeroplanes leave tracks curving like rough wheel tracks in snow — I had a dream this morning that I have forgot but Mother was in distress. All day loading shells from old position — sat doing nothing till I got damned philosophical and sad. Thorburn dreamt 2 nights ago that a maid was counting forks and spoons and he asked her 'Must an officer be present?'*
> *Letter to Helen. Tired still.*
>
> *29. Wet again. Getting refuge trenches dug for detachments. Marking crests on map. How beautiful, like a great crystal sparkling and spangling, the light reflected from some glass which is visible at certain places and times through a hole in cathedral wall, ruined cathedral.*
>
> *30. Bright early, then rain. New zero line, planting pickets. Arranging for material for new O.P. dugout — old one fell in yesterday. Clear and bright and still from 6 p.m. on. Air full of planes and sound of whistles against Hun planes. Blackbirds singing and then chuckling as they go to roost. Two shells falling near Agny Chateau scatter them. Letters from Helen and Mother and parcels from Mother and Eleanor. Too late to bed and had no sleep at all, for the firing, chiefly 60-pounders of our own. Shakespeare's plays for 10 minutes before sleep.*
>
> *31. Up at 5 worn out and wretched. 5.9s flopping on Achicourt while I dressed. Up to Beaurains. There is a chalk-stone cellar with a dripping Bosch dug-out far under and by the last layer of stones is the lilac bush, rather short.*

Suggested Response

1) The passage is part of a personal diary. It mentions events in note form, and reports on similar information such as the weather, and the writing of letters, in each entry. We can assume the numbers correspond to dates.

2) The purpose of the writing seems to be to keep a personal record of daily events. It may not be intended for anyone else to read, but as the writer is involved in a war, he might intend his diary to be read by a friend or relative if he is killed. He might also be writing it to pass the time, as he also spends time reading and writing, perhaps to take his mind off horrifying events.

Did you ask yourself how this war diary came to be published?
You should now be asking yourself whether the writer of the diary was killed, and why his diary should be of interest to a public audience. The diary may have value as a historical document, or it may be of interest if the man who wrote it was famous for some reason.

3) You will have found a number of difficult words. Some are place names which may be unfamiliar to you: *Agny Chateau; Beaurains; Achicourt*.

Some are specialist vocabulary: *Decanille truck; nightlines; detachments; 60-pounders; 5.9s*. These are all terms connected with warfare and weapons.

Some are slang: *Hun; Bosch*. Both these terms are slang used by the British in the 1914-18 war for Germans.

4) The writing is organised into sections which begin with a number. We can guess that each section is the diary entry for one day. The numbers at the beginning of each section are the dates.

5) The writer's attitude seems to be calm and objective (factual) when describing events, but at times he expresses strong emotions: *'-sat doing nothing till I got dammed philosophical and sad'* (entry 28).

However, most of the time he does not directly show an emotional attitude towards the events he reports. The war diary from which you have just read an extract was written by Edward Thomas, a poet and writer.

The entries in his diary are made up of a number of different elements and although his diary was written in dangerous circumstances these elements are the same as in many ordinary diaries.

They are:
1. Reporting of routine, everyday activities.
2. Vivid descriptions or things seen, perhaps the language equivalent of photographs.
3. References to the writer's physical state.
4. Indications of the writer's feelings.

Task: Structuring Diary Entries

Re-read the extracts from Edward Thomas's war diary.

Find and quote an example of:

1) Routine reporting

2) Vivid description

3) References to the writer's physical state

4) Indications of the writer's feelings

When you have written down an example for each of 1-4, turn to the diary extract for the thirtieth of the month (30).

Write down in a column list each 'sentence'* in the section. Next to each one, indicate by number (1, 2, 3 or 4) which function it has:

For example,

Bright early, then rain. ....1 (Routine reporting)

New zero line, planting pickets. ...1

If you think that two functions are being served, then write two numbers next to the 'sentence'.

* These are not grammatically correct sentences, as they are notes which miss out words for the sake of economy. This kind of writing would be incorrect in many circumstances, such as a discussion essay or in a full-length descriptive essay, but it is appropriate for a diary.

Suggested Response to Task: Structuring Diary Entries

There are many examples of **routine reporting**. Here are some:
'Rain and sleet and sun, getting guns camouflaged,
stealing a Decanville truck, laying out nightlines.'
'Letters from Hodson, Eleanor and Sgt. Pellissier.'
'Letters to Helen and Eleanor.'
'Wet again.'
'Getting refuge trenches dug for detachments.'
'Marking crests on map.'

Within his writing, Thomas relies on the use of routine reporting. He comments on the weather '*Rain and sleet and sun*', lists who he has sent and received letters from and discusses activities, such as '*Marking crests on map.*'

Here are some examples of **vivid description**:
Entry 28, from '*Frosty and clear...*' to '*...rough wheel tracks in snow*'.
'*How beautiful, like a great crystal sparkling and spangling, the light reflected from some glass which is visible at certain places and times through a hole in cathedral wall...*'.

The writer engages the reader in his situation through his use of vivid description. He not only comments on the weather but makes careful observations of '*...rough wheel tracks in snow*'.

In the midst of war, he can still see beauty, as when he describes reflected light as '*beautiful, like a great crystal sparkling and spangling*'.

Here are some examples of references to **the writer's physical state:**
'*Still that aching below the nape of my neck...*'
'*Tired still.*'
'*Up at 5 worn out and wretched.*'

He also notes details of his changing physical state. He comments on aches and pains, recording an '*aching below the nape of my neck...*' and providing a sense of permanent exhaustion as he uses minor sentences to record that he is '*Tired still.*' There is a sense of his fatigue as he feels the effects of early mornings ('*Up at 5 worn out and wretched*'). His use of alliteration in this statement hints at his literary background.

Here are some examples of indications of **the writer's feelings:**
'*I had a dream this morning... in distress*'
'*-sat doing nothing till I got damned philosophical and sad.*'
'*Up at 5 worn out and wretched*'.

Despite its brief and factual style, there are moments where the writer reflects upon his feelings and emotions: he wakes from his dreams '*in distress*'; the lack of activity breeds depression as he recalls how he '*-sat doing nothing till I got damned philosophical and sad.*'

Read the following report of events carefully. Your task will be to convert it into the style of a diary entry, like those you have read from Edward Thomas's war diary:

> 'On the fourth of April, I got up at half-past four in the morning. I heard some blackbirds singing at the battery at a quarter to six, but then the shooting began at half past. The morning was cloudy and fresh, although later on it turned showery and cold, making the ground muddy and slippery underfoot. We fired off six hundred rounds and as yet there has been nothing fired in return. By a quarter past nine I felt tired and I moved to the dugout in the position.
>
> 'A letter from Helen arrived today. Tonight the sound of the artillery is making the air flap all night long.'

Task: Narrative in Diary Form

Re-write this account of one day's experiences in diary form. You should take into consideration the following:

• Refer back to the diary entries you have read.

• Note the way dates, times and numbers are written using figures, not words.

• Note the way the writer describes his actions. He misses out the personal pronoun 'I', and uses the present participle '...ing' to indicate activities over which he spent some time. For example:

'getting refuge trenches dug'; 'laying out night lines'

• He misses out the verb 'to be'. Instead of saying 'I was tired' or

'It was wet', he says 'tired' and 'wet'.

• You should use short sentences or phrases.

• Be as concise as possible; be economical in your use of words and say things as briefly as possible.

Remember, you are writing a diary entry for an exhausting day in the front line of battle.

Suggested Response to Task: Narrative in Diary Form

When you are sure you have finished, read the diary entry written by Edward Thomas for April 4th 1917:

> '4. Up at 4.30. Blackbirds sing at battery at 5.45 – shooting at 6.30.
>
> A cloudy fresh morning. But showery cold muddy and slippery later.
>
> 600 rounds. Nothing in return yet. Tired by 9.15 p.m. Moved to dugout in position. Letter from Helen. Artillery makes air flap all night long.'

By writing in the appropriate format and style for a diary, you have learnt how information and ideas can be written in an economical way. The way a diary is written may seem similar to the way a student takes notes. Like notes, a diary can be used by a writer to store ideas, impressions and information. This store can be used later to provide the raw material for writing that is more carefully shaped and organised, such as prose or poetry.

In the examination, it may be appropriate to use elements of diary or journal form but try to avoid the shorthand and condensed grammar Thomas employs.

When Edward Thomas wrote his diary, he was trying to record all the things he noticed and wanted to remember. The order in which he wrote things down did not matter as much as quick accurate description of details. When he wrote his famous poem *Adlestrop*, he was trying to make the person reading it feel as though they were there, so he began with the arrival at the station, then the platform, then the surrounding fields, then the sky, then the birdsong.

It is not very difficult to tell the difference between poems written by Thomas and the diary entry, but it is more difficult to tell the difference between part of a diary, and part of a story. The key to telling the difference is the different purpose for which diaries and stories are written, and the different effect they have on their readers.

The two pieces of writing below are both about the experiences of soldiers directly involved in the day-to-day events of warfare. As you read them, ask yourself if we can tell whether they are:

(a) Extracts from diaries

(b) Based on personal experience.

Extract A

I jumped up on the fire-step beside the sentry and cautiously raised my head, staring over the parapet. I could see nothing except the wooden pickets supporting our protecting barbed-wire entanglements, and a dark patch or two of bushes beyond. The darkness seemed to move and shake about as I looked at it; the bushes started travelling, singly at first, then both together. The pickets did the same. I was glad of the sentry beside me; he gave his name as Beaumont. 'They're quiet tonight sir,' he said. 'A relief going on; I think so, surely.' I said: 'It's funny how those bushes seem to move.'

'Aye, they do play queer tricks. Is this your first spell in trenches, sir?' A German flare shot up, broke into bright flame, dropped slowly and went hissing into the grass just behind our trench, showing up the bushes and pickets. Instinctively I moved.

Extract B

The cold passed reluctantly from the earth, and the retiring fogs revealed an army stretched out on the hills, resting. As the landscape changed from brown to green, the army awakened, and began to tremble with eagerness at the noise of rumours. It cast its eyes upon the roads, which were growing from long troughs of liquid mud to proper thorough-fares. A river, amber-tinted in the shadow of its banks, purled at the army's feet; and at night, when the stream had become of a sorrowful blackness, one could see across it the red, eyelike gleam of hostile camp-fires set in the low brows of distant hills.

Task: Writing for different purposes

Texts are organised in different ways depending on the different purposes for which they are written.

In order to record and organise your observations on the two passages A and B, fill out the table below:

	A Yes/No	B Yes/No
Has this been written as a series of economical notes?		
Does this piece of writing try to make the reader feel as though he/she is actually watching of participating in events?		
Does the writing mix up the reporting of everyday events with more personal observations?		
Could this much detail or dialogue be noted down at the time or accurately remembered later that day?		
Is it likely that the writer supplied some details from imagination?		
Are the descriptions of landscape and surroundings carefully organised?		
Does the writer talk about events as if he is taking part in them?		
Does the writer have a 'bird's-eye' view, overlooking what is described?		

Suggested Response to Task: Writing for Different Purposes

It is often not possible to tell whether a piece of writing is based on personal experience, but we can be sure that even if these two pieces are based on personal experience, the writer of each one has carefully shaped, organised and even invented details. The writer of piece A wants the reader to be involved in the action described, and see things from the point of view of the narrator. The writer of piece B wants the reader to visualise the scene that is described, as though the reader were looking down on it from above.

Passage A is from *Goodbye to All That,* by Robert Graves, which is an autobiography. So Passage A is based on personal experience, but it is not a diary, and it is difficult to believe that the writer could have recorded the precise details and dialogue in the extract. It is probable that he 'fleshed out' the story by inventing details that he could not precisely remember.

Passage B is from *The Red Badge of Courage,* by Stephen Crane. Whereas Graves and Thomas wrote about the 1914-18 war, on the basis of their own experiences, Stephen Crane wrote about the American Civil War, which was over shortly before he was born. *The Red Badge of Courage* is a novel that is not based on personal experience, but the author makes his fiction very real and convincing to the reader.

Point of View

You have looked at how the shaping and organisation of writing about personal experience varies according to whether the writer is recording facts, or seeking to create feelings and events for the reader to imagine. In this section of the section you will be looking at writing in which the same events are described from the point of view of different speakers. You will be learning how the writer's choice of point of view affects the details and the shaping of his/her account of events.

Aspects of Narrative Writing

There are four main types of writing you might expect to find in a prose novel: narrative, description, dialogue and thoughts.

Narrative Writing

Narrative writing 'tells the story', as in the following extract:

Madison rang the doorbell, stamping his feet against the cold. No response. He tried again, taking a couple of steps sideways to peer through the window. Again, no one answered. Pulling his scarf up around his ears, he let himself in through the side gate and walked round to the back garden. He pressed his face against the kitchen window. The dog leapt up, yelping and scratching at the door. Madison's gaze travelled across the room. He gasped as he saw Mrs. Turner. She lay motionless on the floor, one leg twisted under her body, her arms thrown up around her head as if to protect herself.

Description

Descriptive writing tells us what people, places and things are like. Here is an extract from a nineteenth century text by Charles Dickens:

The scene was a plain, bare, monotonous vault of a schoolroom, and the speaker's square forefinger emphasised his observations by underscoring every sentence with a line on the schoolmaster's sleeve. The emphasis was helped by the speaker's square wall of a forehead, which had his eyebrows for its base, while his eyes found commodious cellarage in two dark caves, overshadowed by the wall. The emphasis was helped by the speaker's mouth, which was wide, thin, and hard set. The emphasis was helped by the speaker's voice, which was inflexible, dry and dictatorial. The emphasis was helped by the speaker's hair, which bristled on the skirts of his bald head, a plantation of firs to keep the wind from its shining surface, all covered with knobs, like the crust of a plum pie, as if the head had scarcely warehouse-room for the hard facts stored inside. The speaker's obstinate carriage, square coat, square legs, square shoulders – nay, his very neck cloth, trained to take him by the throat with an unaccommodating grasp, like a stubborn fact, as it was – all helped the emphasis.

Note how the use of carefully selected adjectives before nouns helps to support the view that this character is stern and unfriendly. When developing your own written work you should aim to think about how you can use a wider vocabulary for emphasis and effect. Written work can sometimes be let down by not using a wide enough range of vocabulary. Careful planning can help maintain variety in your writing.

Synonyms are words with similar meanings. For example, the words *small, little, tiny* and *minute* are synonyms. They have similar but not exactly the same meanings.

One 'repeat offender' In GCSE responses can be the reliance on words like 'nice' to describe things when more often than not there are many better and more specific alternatives that can convey the writer's ideas more effectively.

Never be nice! Far better to be *agreeable, attractive, charming, delicate, delightful, fine, friendly, good, kind, likeable, neat, pleasant, polite, precise, refined, respectable, tidy, virtuous, well-mannered.*

Another technique which can make descriptive and creative writing lively is the use of **figurative language**. We have already discusses two of the most familiar methods, similes and metaphors.

To briefly recap, a **simile** compares one item with another. It can usually be identified by the use of the words 'as' or 'like' which are used to bring the two ideas together. It is worth noting that when using similes it is important to avoid clichés or well-worn phrases, such as saying someone is *'good as gold'*.

Like a simile, a **metaphor** compares an object, person or animal with another item. Instead of saying that something is 'like' or 'as' something else, a metaphor says that it is something else.

Read the extract – also from Dickens - below and identify his use of simile and metaphor to create a strong sense of place.

It was a town of red brick, or of brick that would have been red if the smoke and ashes had allowed it but as matters stood it was a town of unnatural red and black like the painted face of a savage. It was a town of machinery and tall chimneys, out of which interminable serpents of smoke trailed themselves for ever and ever, and never got uncoiled. It had a black canal in it, and a river that ran purple with ill-smelling dye, arid vast piles of building full of windows where there was a rattling and a trembling all day long, and where the piston of the steam-engine worked monotonously up and down, like the head of an elephant in a state of melancholy madness. It contained several large streets all very like one another, and many small streets still more like one another, inhabited by people equally like one another, who all went in and out at the same hours, with the same sound upon the same pavements, to do the same work, and to whom every day was the same as yesterday and tomorrow, and every year the counterpart of the last and the next...

The discolouration of the buildings is like' a *'painted face'* while the chimneys belch out' *serpents of smoke'*. The steam piston moves *'like the head of an elephant'*. His similes make comparisons with physical characteristics and actions, while the metaphor insinuates that the factories will eventually harm or threaten the people, as a snake might. Compound adjectives increase the sense of disgust, as when the river runs purple with *'ill-smelling dye'*. The end of the passage makes use of repetition to suggest monotony and a lack of identity as people and places are *'like one another'* as they do the *'same'* thing every day, year in, year out.

Dialogue

Dialogue is the use of conversation between characters in a novel or story. It can add interest and provide another way of conveying aspects of character. In the short example below, from a modern example, you can sense the tension between the two characters, and the unnamed speaker's urgent plea to Emma to continue with the plan.

'What's the point?'. Emma was sprawled across the bed, arms behind her head, eyes half closed.
'What's the point? If you're going to take that attitude, what's the point in us being here at all? What's the point in us spending a year on the run, never seeing our families, living in constant fear? The point, Emma, is that if we give up now, they've won. Then what would the point be?'
Emma turned away, mumbling something into the pillow.
'What? I can't hear you.'
She turned back, her face tired and drawn. 'I'm just so sick of it all. Sometimes I wonder if it wouldn't have been better just to give ourselves up in the first place. Get it over with. They'd probably have given us six months at the most. We'd be free again by now.

Conveying Thoughts: Interior Monologue

The writer sometimes tells us what a character is thinking. In the extract below the description moves between the emotional response to the activity and the reflection on her reaction to another character:

There was something about the rhythm of the strokes, the repetitive pattern of swimming up and down the pool, the gentle splash of water mixed with the distorted underwater sounds, that cut through the woolliness in her head.
Damn James! Just when everything was beginning to come together, trust him to show up and turn it all upside down again. If only she'd known he was coming she could have prepared herself, arranged to be out all week, prove to him that she could build a full and happy life without him. But turning up on her doorstep unannounced with a big grin and a bunch of flowers – that was so typical of James. She wasn't going to fall for it again, she wasn't!

Task: Narrative Writing

The following extract is taken from a key turning point in the novel *Lord of the Flies* by William Golding. In this novel, a group of young boys have been marooned on an island without any adults. First read the extract, then consider the questions on narrative techniques below.

The boys have tried to establish a society, although there has been conflict between the quieter boys, who want to plan survival as a group, and the boys who follow the influential Jack, calling themselves the hunters. In this extract Jack's hunters and the smaller boys are caught in a storm. The boys are becoming increasingly excited in their quest for the pig. The quiet and peaceful Simon is returning to camp with news about the dead airman they have discovered, and he enters the frenzied scene, with horrific consequences.

Part A: Writer's Craft
Setting and Establishing Scene
1. Describe the setting. How does the author use the setting to establish the story?
Plot
2. This passage is a key point in the story. How does the writer suggest what might happen next?
Character
3. (a) How many significant characters are mentioned and who is/are the major character(s)? (b) What do we learn about the major characters?
Dialogue
4. What does the dialogue add to the story? What do we learn from it?
Part B: Imaginative Writing
Write the next part of the story.

The hunters were looking uneasily at the sky, flinching from the stroke of the drops. A wave of restlessness set the boys swaying and moving aimlessly.

The flickering light became brighter and the blows of the thunder were only just bearable. The littluns began to run about, screaming. Jack leapt on to the sand.

"Do our dance! Come on! Dance!"

He ran stumbling through the thick sand to the open space of rock beyond the fire. Between the flashes of lightning the air was dark and terrible; and the boys followed him, clamorously. Roger became the pig, grunting and charging at Jack, who side-stepped. The hunters took their spears, the cooks took spits, and the rest clubs of firewood. A circling movement developed and a chant. While Roger mimed the terror of the pig, the littluns ran and jumped on the outside of the circle. Piggy and Ralph, under the threat of the sky, found themselves eager to take a place in this demented but partly secure society. They were glad to touch the brown backs of the fence that hemmed in the terror and made it governable.

"Kill the beast! Cut his throat! Spill his blood!"

The movement became regular while the chant lost its first superficial excitement and began to beat like a steady pulse. Roger ceased to be a pig and became a hunter, so that the center of the ring yawned emptily.

Some of the littluns started a ring on their own; and the complementary circles went round and round as though repetition would achieve safety of itself. There was the throb and stamp of a single organism.

The dark sky was shattered by a blue-white scar. An instant later the noise was on them like the blow of a gigantic whip. The chant rose a tone in agony.

"Kill the beast! Cut his throat! Spill his blood!"

Now out of the terror rose another desire, thick, urgent, blind.

"Kill the beast! Cut his throat! Spill his blood!"

Again the blue-white scar jagged above them and the sulphurous explosion beat down. The littluns screamed and blundered about, fleeing from the edge of the forest, and one of them broke the ring of biguns in his terror.

"Him! Him!"

The circle became a horseshoe. A thing was crawling out of the forest.

It came darkly, uncertainly. The shrill screaming that rose before the beast was like a pain. The beast stumbled into the horseshoe.

"Kill the beast! Cut his throat! Spill his blood!"

The blue-white scar was constant, the noise unendurable. Simon was crying out something about a dead man on a hill.

"Kill the beast! Cut his throat! Spill his blood! Do him in!"

The sticks fell and the mouth of the new circle crunched and screamed.

The beast was on its knees in the center, its arms folded over its face. It was crying out against the abominable noise something about a body on the hill. The beast struggled forward, broke the ring and fell over the steep edge of the rock to the sand by the water. At once the crowd surged after it, poured down the rock, leapt on to the beast, screamed, struck, bit, tore. There were no words, and no movements but the tearing of teeth and claws.

Then the clouds opened and let down the rain like a waterfall. The water bounded from the mountain-top, tore leaves and branches from the trees, poured like a cold shower over the struggling heap on the sand.

Presently the heap broke up and figures staggered away. Only the beast lay still, a few yards from the sea. Even in the rain they could see how small a beast it was; and already its blood was staining the sand.

Now a great wind blew the rain sideways, cascading the water from the forest trees. On the mountain-top the parachute filled and moved; the figure slid, rose to its feet, spun, swayed down through a vastness of wet air and trod with ungainly feet the tops of the high trees; falling, still falling, it sank toward the beach and the boys rushed screaming into the darkness. The parachute took the figure forward, furrowing the lagoon, and bumped it over the reef and out to sea.

Towards midnight the rain ceased and the clouds drifted away, so that the sky was scattered once more with the incredible lamps of stars. Then the breeze died too and there was no noise save the drip and trickle of water that ran out of clefts and spilled down, leaf by leaf, to the brown earth of the island. The air was cool, moist, and clear; and presently even the sound of the water was still. The beast lay huddled on the pale beach and the stains spread, inch by inch.

The edge of the lagoon became a streak of phosphorescence which advanced minutely, as the great wave of the tide flowed. The clear water mirrored the clear sky and the angular bright constellations. The line of phosphorescence bulged about the sand grains and little pebbles; it held them each in a dimple of tension, then suddenly accepted them with an inaudible syllable and moved on.

Along the shoreward edge of the shallows the advancing clearness was full of strange, moonbeam-bodied creatures with fiery eyes. Here and there a larger pebble clung to its own air and was covered with a coat of pearls. The tide swelled in over the rain-pitted sand and smoothed everything with a layer of silver. Now it touched the first of the stains that seeped from the broken body and the creatures made a moving patch of light as they gathered at the edge. The water rose farther and dressed Simon's coarse hair with brightness. The line of his cheek silvered and the turn of his shoulder became sculptured marble. The strange attendant creatures, with their fiery eyes and trailing vapors, busied themselves round his head. The body lifted a fraction of an inch from the sand and a bubble of air escaped from the mouth with a wet plop. Then it turned gently in the water.

Somewhere over the darkened curve of the world the sun and moon were pulling, and the film of water on the earth planet was held, bulging slightly on one side while the solid core turned. The great wave of the tide moved farther along the island and the water lifted. Softly, surrounded by a fringe of inquisitive bright creatures, itself a silver shape beneath the steadfast constellations, Simon's dead body moved out toward the open sea.

Suggested Response to Task: Narrative Writing

Part A: Writer's Craft

Setting and Establishing Scene

The physical surroundings are sketched in a straightforward way – we know the boys are dancing around a fire and that they are near a rock. Pathetic fallacy is a key device in this passage. The sights and sounds of the thunderstorm are described in detail. *'The blows of the thunder'* are personified while the lightning becomes a *'sulphurous explosion'*. This creates a hellish scene and prepares for the violence to come.

Plot

The choice of nouns is key here. No longer referred to as boys, the passage begins by detailing the movements of *'the hunters'*. Roger and Jack are miming a hunter and a pig, while Piggy and Ralph, who seem weaker due to being *'eager'* to join in, note that the behaviour of the group is becoming *'demented'*.

Roger stops pretending to be a pig, leaving the circle empty. The chants to 'Kill the beast' become louder. There is suspense as *'A thing was crawling out of the forest'*. The writer briefly refers to a boy called Simon crying about a man. At the same time, all the boys are beating and stabbing *'the beast'* from the forest with sticks. The reader is shocked by the detail that it had *'its arms folded over its face'*. There is confusion and cries about a body on the hill, revealing that the boys are not attacking a pig, but may be beating Simon. The horror continues as what they believe to be the *'beast'* is forced over s steep rock onto the beach below. Working as a group, they continue the savagery:

At once the crowd surged after it, poured down the rock, leapt on to the beast, screamed, struck, bit, tore. There were no words, and no movements but the tearing of teeth and claws.

The text continues to refer to the beast until the close of the extract where the 'broken body' is revealed to be *'Simon's dead body'*, floating out to sea in the moonlight.

Character

This is an interesting passage in that the focus is on group mentality rather than individual characters. There is some differentiation, with Jack and

Roger clearly influential leaders of the 'littluns' while Piggy and Ralph copy the group. Simon is singled out as the victim although the power of the passage comes in the skilful alteration between naming Simon and making reference to 'the beast'. In the confusion of the storm and the frenzy of the hunt the boys have ceased to have individual responsibility and have committed a brutal murder.

Dialogue

There is limited dialogue in the passage but the reader learns that Jack commands the group to *'Dance'*. The chant of *'Kill the best! Cut his throat! Spill his blood!'* is repeated like a refrain through the extract, becoming louder. There is a clue that there is some awareness of what they are doing when the smaller boys come shrieking from the forest *'Him! Him!'*. This indicates they have some realisation that they are not attacking an animal. Simon's speech is reported rather than presented as direct speech. This is a critical decision as direct speech would have suggested the boys would have to acknowledge they were attacking a human being. The references to Simon's cries convey the confusion of the scene and the possibility that the boys have made a genuine mistake.

Part B: Imaginative Writing

When using existing prose fiction or poetry texts as a source for your imaginative writing, do not be afraid to take your text in a different direction from the original source. Here, your focus would probably be on the aftermath of Simon's death and the respective actions and reactions of the boys.

While you had limited background information on the individual characters you may have decided to have Jack and Roger react in a defensive way, trying to justify the killing, while Ralph and Piggy may have been more fearful or guilty. The smaller boys may be presented as more upset, or possibility lacking the full understanding of what they have done.

In the original novel, the boys are eventually discovered by a naval officer who has arrived with a rescue ship. He mistakenly believes they are indulging in childish games of dressing-up, and seems unaware of the bullying and violence which has infected the group. In your writing, you may well have introduced an adult or outsider who has discovered the body and is now deciding on a suitable punishment.

2.5 The Writer's Toolkit

This section will help you to;

- Consider the skills required for imaginative writing
- Distinguish between alternative forms of written English
- Communicate effectively, adapting form, tone and register of writing for specific purposes and audiences
- Write clearly, using a range of vocabulary and sentence structures
- Use appropriate paragraphing and accurate spelling, grammar and punctuation.
- Write convincingly about imaginary experiences
- Analyse a literary passage in some detail
- Present dialogue and find suitable speech patterns for different characters

The Writer's Toolkit

Writing to explore, imagine and entertain

1. Write with clarity

Avoid clumsy sentences, flowery language, red herrings, and too much description. Keep it clear and simple. Let the reader get on with the story.

2. Balance 'show' and 'tell'

In the main, use concrete description rather than telling the reader what to think or feel.

3. Don't overload the reader

Do not labour description - often one or two details that suggest character or setting will be sufficient. The reader can infer from their imagination.

4. Use hooks and links

Tease the reader by dropping in hints and suggestions. Make sure that there are sufficient links to keep the narrative fluid.

5. Build pictures with sense impressions

Concrete description helps the reader to live the story by creating images.

6. Be natural

Use the flow of your own language. Avoid trying to be too clever, flowery or literary.

7. 'Get in, get on, get out'

Raymond Carver said this. Let the narrative drive the writing.

Developing Vocabulary

1. Strengthen nouns and verbs

Use precise nouns as they have strong connotations - use powerful verbs as they suggest how characters feel, Rather than write *'The man got in the car'* consider *'Michael slithered into the Mercedes'* to suggest suspicious behaviour.

2. Beware of unnecessary modification

While they can add nuances to your writing, take care when you use an adjective or adverb that these are not used to support a weak noun or verb. Avoid overwriting.

3. Keep it simple and powerful

Do not use extra words or sentences. These will slow up the narrative. 'Empty' words can create suspense, as in the use of 'thing' in the passage from *Lord of the Flies.*

4. Tighten sentences

Keep an eye on making your sentences dramatic. Should you write *'The man was running down the lane'* or *'The man ran'*, if you are trying to create tension?

5. Be wary of abstractions

Ezra Pound said this. Avoid writing complex abstractions. This can lose the reader. Keep the writing concrete.

6. Choose the right language

For example, to create suspense, words such as suddenly or without warning may help.

Thinking about narrative - Creating sentences:

1. Vary sentences

Balance the rhythm of short/long sentences. Use simple sentences for clarity and impact. Use compound for flow. Use complex to add extra layers of meaning. Do you want to use questions to draw the reader into the narrative? Exclamations command attention!

2. Use sentence fragments (also known as 'minor sentences')

Break the sentence rule, using a fragment to emphasise a point. Sparingly.

3. Vary sentence openings

Starting every sentence in the same way is dull. Experiment with adverbs (***Carefully***, she...), non-finite verbs (**Laughing**, she... or **Startled**, he...), prepositional phrases (**At the end** of the street, ...), similes (**Like a train**, she ran), subordinate clauses ***(Although*** she was tired,...).

4. Vary word order

Consider the impact on meaning of varying word order. *Around the edges, a crowd had gathered.*

5. Add in and on

Add in words, phrases or clauses to include extra information that is needed, Example: *The man, who had been shot, climbed into the car.* Or add on at the end, or beginning, of the sentence to extend what you are saying, Example: *After eating, the man climbed into the car and settled down to sleep.*

6. Intensify sentences

Change words to intensify meaning - *'The girl went home'* is less effective than *'Rachel limped home'*.

7. Use stylistic devices sparingly

Create sounds with alliteration and onomatopoeia. Create images with similes, metaphors and personification.

8. Trim it back

Cut sentences back for impact.

9. Use sentences to intrigue the reader

She knew she was dead...

Sample Assessment Tasks: Paper 2 Section B Imaginative Writing

EITHER

Write a story with the title *'The Visitor'*.

Your response could be real or imagined.

OR

Write a story which ends: *'It was difficult to look back without feeling a sense of regret.'*

Your response could be real or imagined.

EITHER

Write about a time when you, or someone you know, had an **unexpected experience.**

Your response could be real or imagined.

OR

Write a story with the title 'Left Behind'.

Your response could be real or imagined.

OR

Write a story that begins 'I wanted to make my own decision'.

Your response could be real or imagined.

There is a total of **30 marks** for the Imaginative Writing Response.

18 marks are awarded for effective use of writing techniques with **12 marks** available for technical accuracy. You should use the performance grids on the following pages to review and assess your own writing.

AO4 COMMUNICATE EFFECTIVELY AND IMAGINATIVELY

Communicate effectively and imaginatively, adapting form, tone and register of writing for specific purposes and audiences

Level 1 1–3

- Communication is at a **basic** level, and **limited** in clarity.
- **Little awareness** is shown of the purpose of the writing and the intended reader.
- **Little awareness** of form, tone and register.

Level 2 4–7

- Communicates in a **broadly appropriate** way.
- Shows **some grasp** of the purpose and of the expectations/ requirements of the intended reader.
- **Straightforward use** of form, tone and register.

Level 3 8–11

- Communicates **clearly**.
- **Generally clear** sense of purpose and understanding of the expectations/requirements of the intended reader.
- **Appropriate use** of form, tone and register.

Level 4 12–15

- Communicates **successfully**.
- **A secure realisation** of the writing task according to the writer's purpose and the expectations/requirements of the intended reader is shown.
- **Effective use** of form, tone and register.

Level 5 16–18

- Communication is **perceptive and subtle** with discriminating use of a full vocabulary.
- Task is **sharply focused** on purpose and the expectations/requirements of the intended reader.
- **Sophisticated control** of text structure, skilfully sustained paragraphing as appropriate and/or assured application of a range of cohesive devices.

AO5 WRITE CLEARLY AND ACCURATELY

Write clearly, using a range of vocabulary and sentence structures, with appropriate paragraphing and accurate spelling, grammar and punctuation

Level 1 1–2

- Expresses information and ideas, with limited use of structural and grammatical features.
- Uses basic vocabulary, often misspelt.
- Uses punctuation with **basic control,** creating undeveloped, often repetitive, sentence structures.

Level 2 3–4

- **Expresses and orders** information and ideas; uses paragraphs and a range of structural and grammatical features.
- Writes with **some correctly spelt** vocabulary, e.g. words with regular patterns such as prefixes, suffixes, double consonants.
- Uses punctuation with **some control,** creating a range of sentence structures, including coordination and subordination.

Level 3 5–7

- **Develops and connects** appropriate information and ideas; structural and grammatical features and paragraphing make the meaning clear.
- Uses a **varied vocabulary** and spells words containing irregular patterns correctly.
- Uses **accurate and varied** punctuation, adapting sentence structure as appropriate.

Level 4 8–10

- **Manages information and ideas,** with structural and grammatical features used cohesively and deliberately across the text.
- Uses a wide, selective vocabulary with only occasional spelling errors.
- Positions a **range of punctuation** for clarity, managing sentence structures for deliberate effect.

Level 5 11–12

- **Manipulates complex ideas,** utilising a range of structural and grammatical features to support coherence and cohesion.
- Uses **extensive vocabulary** strategically; rare spelling errors do not detract from overall meaning.
- **Punctuates writing with accuracy** to aid emphasis and precision, using a range of sentence structures accurately and selectively, to achieve particular effects.

Key Terms Glossary

adjective	Words used to describe nouns.
adverb	These modify verbs and tell us how something is or was done.
allegory	A literary technique which presents abstract ideas and values through recognisable characters, figures and events.
alliteration	The repetition of the same or similar sounds at the beginning of words or in stressed syllables of a phrase. This is often indicated by a repeated letter pattern, but this is not always the case.
allusion	An indirect reference to a person, place or event. This can be fictional or real.
anaphora	The repetition of a word or phrase at the beginning of a sentence, clause or verse.
Anthropomorphism	The linking of human characteristics or behaviour to an animal, god or object.
antithesis	The presentation of a person or object as the direct opposite of a person or object.
apostrophe	A rhetorical device. An exclamatory passage (sometimes indicated by "O!") in a speech or poem addressed to a person or thing.
archaic	Old-fashioned language, no longer in everyday use.
archetype/ archetypal	Typical of a type of person or thing.
cliché	A predictable or unoriginal phrase or idea.
collocation	A pair or group of words that are regularly used together ('fish and chips').
colloquial	Informal language used in normal or everyday conversation. It does not seem literary.
conjunction	Words that link two parts of a sentence or two or more sentences together.
connotation	An idea or feeling which a word suggests to a reader in addition to its main meaning.
declarative	A sentence taking the form of a simple statement.
ellipsis	The exclusion from speech or writing of a word or words that can be understood from the context of the remaining text. Indicated by …
enjambment	In poetry, this is a sentence which continues without a pause beyond the end of a line, stanza or couplet.
epilogue	A section that serves as a comment or conclusion relating to the text.
foreshadowing	An element serving as a warning or caution for a future event.

fricative	A consonant sound made by the friction of breath.
idiom	An expression where meaning cannot be deduced from individual words e.g. *it's raining cats and dogs*.
imagery	Visually descriptive language.
imperative	An authoritative command.
irony	The use of words to convey a meaning that is the opposite of its literal meaning
Juxtaposition	A device where two elements are placed close together with contrasting effect.
lexis	Words in a language. In analysis, this refers to vocabulary choices.
listing	The use of a list for emphasis or effect. Also **tri-colon or tripartite listing** which uses a list of three for emphasis.
Metaphor	A device whereby one thing is used to represent or symbolise something else. An extended metaphor is one which is developed over a section of the text or the whole text.
microcosm	A place or situation which reflects the characteristics of something much larger.
onomatopoeia	A word that is formed from the sound associated with what it names e.g. Tick-tock
personification	Giving a non-human animal or object a personal nature or human characteristics, or representing abstract qualities in human form e.g. Faith and Hope as female forms
plosive	Consonant sound made by stopping then suddenly releasing air.
pre-modification	Additional information provided before the noun, usually by an adjective.
proper noun	Name used for an individual place, person or organisation.
register	The level or pitch of the language e.g. informal register to suggest a close relationship
repetition	Repeating words or sounds for deliberate effect.
rhetoric	the art of using persuasive language devices
simile	Comparing one thing to another, using like or as, to create a vivid image.
symbol	Something used to represent a larger idea or concept.
syntax	Arrangement of words or phrases within a sentence.
sound pattern	This is a deliberate organisation of words to create specific sound effects.
tone	The general attitude of a piece of writing; the sense of mood or feeling.
verb	A word describing an action or state.

Printed in Great Britain
by Amazon